ARNOLD SCHWARZENEGGER

ARNOLD SCHWARZENEGGER

A Biography

Louise Krasniewicz and Michael Blitz

GREENWOOD BIOGRAPHIES

GREENWOOD PRESS
WESTPORT, CONNECTICUT • LONDON

Library of Congress Cataloging-in-Publication Data

Krasniewicz, Louise, 1952–
    Arnold Schwarzenegger : a biography / Louise Krasniewicz and Michael Blitz.
       p. cm.—(Greenwood biographies ISSN 1540–4900)
    Includes bibliographical references and index.
    ISBN 0–313–33810–8
    1. Schwarzenegger, Arnold. 2. Bodybuilders—United States—Biography.
3. Actors—United States—Biography. 4. Celebrities—United States—
Biography. 5. Governors—California—Biography. I. Blitz, Michael. II. Title.
    GV545.52.S38K73   2006
    796.41092—dc22[B]   2006025383

British Library Cataloguing in Publication Data is available.

Library of Congress Catalog Card Number: 2006025383
ISBN: 0–313–33810–8
ISSN: 1540–4900

First published in 2006

Greenwood Press, 88 Post Road West, Westport, CT 06881
An imprint of Greenwood Publishing Group, Inc.
www.greenwood.com

Printed in the United States of America

The paper used in this book complies with the
Permanent Paper Standard issued by the National
Information Standards Organization (Z39.48–1984).

10 9 8 7 6 5 4 3 2 1

CONTENTS

SERIES FOREWORD

In response to high school and public library needs, Greenwood developed this distinguished series of full-length biographies specifically for student use. Prepared by field experts and professionals, these engaging biographies are tailored for high school students who need challenging yet accessible biographies. Ideal for secondary school assignments, the length, format and subject areas are designed to meet educators' requirements and students' interests.

Greenwood offers an extensive selection of biographies spanning all curriculum-related subject areas including social studies, the sciences, literature and the arts, history and politics, as well as popular culture, covering public figures and famous personalities from all time periods and backgrounds, both historic and contemporary, who have made an impact on American and/or world culture. Greenwood biographies were chosen based on comprehensive feedback from librarians and educators. Consideration was given to both curriculum relevance and inherent interest. The result is an intriguing mix of the well known and the unexpected, the saints and sinners from long-ago history and contemporary pop culture. Readers will find a wide array of subject choices from fascinating crime figures like Al Capone to inspiring pioneers like Margaret Mead, from the greatest minds of our time like Stephen Hawking to the most amazing success stories of our day like J.K. Rowling.

While the emphasis is on fact, not glorification, the books are meant to be fun to read. Each volume provides in-depth information about the subject's life from birth through childhood, the teen years, and adulthood.

A thorough account relates family background and education, traces personal and professional influences, and explores struggles, accomplishments, and contributions. A timeline highlights the most significant life events against a historical perspective. Bibliographies supplement the reference value of each volume.

ACKNOWLEDGMENTS

Books are always collaborations, whether between writers, writers and research assistants, writers and editors, and writers and their networks of honest readers and critics. This book is the result of collaborations of all kinds. The two of us have written together for more than 20 years; it remains an exciting and joyful intellectual partnership. In doing this biography of Arnold Schwarzenegger, we are grateful for the assistance and support from a number of others: Kristi Ward, our editor at Greenwood, provided encouragement and constructive support from the beginning; colleagues and students at the University of Pennsylvania and John Jay College of Criminal Justice, CUNY were generous in their interest in, and ongoing support of, the work of their resident "Schwarzeneggerologists"; Emily Davis contributed research on Governor Schwarzenegger; our friends and families kept on smiling and encouraging us as we submitted ourselves (and them!) to the rigors of co-authoring another book. For our spouses—Richard Leventhal and Mozelle Dayan-Blitz—we are fortunate beyond measure; for our children—Drew Leventhal, Daina and Cory Blitz, and Celine and Rene Dayan-Bonilla—we are blessed.

INTRODUCTION: INTRODUCING ARNOLD ALOIS SCHWARZENEGGER

Once referred to by fellow bodybuilder Rick Wayne as "the German kid with the overdeveloped name,"[1] Arnold Schwarzenegger, world-famous Austrian (not German), has been among the most significant and influential figures in American popular culture in the late twentieth and early twenty-first centuries. His list of accomplishments and his spheres of influence seem like they belong to three or four people, not just one: movies, business, sports, publishing, public policy, foreign policy, politics, fitness, language, philanthropy, celebrity, history, international relations. It's not his name that is overdeveloped; it is Arnold's career that has developed beyond all ordinary proportions—an incredible progression of milestones along a global superhighway. Arnold's story is a dramatic and fabled rendition of the American Dream.

The American Dream. We will use Arnold's life to explore what it is and if such a thing really exists. Has the American Dream, a set of desires for security, fame, fortune, recognition and power, really been guiding this nation for over 230 years and Arnold Schwarzenegger for most of his life? Does it bring out the best in Americans and all who aspire to be Americans? Is Arnold Schwarzenegger the perfect example of what the American dream has a tendency to produce? We think a story of Arnold's life is a story based on the American Dream: what it is, what it produces, how it works.

How does Arnold demonstrate the American Dream? To start, Arnold Schwarzenegger has gained fame by dominating an individual sport, bodybuilding, like few athletes have, and he also significantly redefined the sport in his own image. By comparison, in basketball we might think of

Wilt Chamberlain, playing 1960 to 1973, who holds almost 100 National Basketball Association records including the first 100 point game or Michael Jordan, who transformed basketball into a form of athletic magic. In golf we could think of Jack Nicklaus, who has won 18 professional tournaments, or in baseball we could look at Hank Aaron, who played from 1954 to 1976 and still holds the record for the most home runs. In many ways, the name Lance Armstrong has become synonymous not only with cycling, but with athletic achievement, in the same way that the Williams sisters have raised women's tennis to new levels of intensity. Skaters like Dorothy Hamill and Peggy Fleming were instrumental in bringing about sweeping changes in the world of figure skating, and for many years Mark Spitz was *the* American swimmer. But none of these figures has ever electrified an entire culture in so wide a variety of ways and then rode that current of excitement into politics and powerful cultural influence. Arnold Schwarzenegger, renowned as the greatest bodybuilder of all time, has also built a reputation as an unstoppable force who continues to fascinate not only sports fans and not only Americans, but people throughout the world.

Many years after he conquered the bodybuilding world, and despite the fact that in some recent photos he seems to have deteriorated into a flabby middle-aged man, he is still referenced as the ideal body, the biggest, the best ever. Even though the flaws of his self-built body were quite obvious as he was originally training—droopy shoulders, weak calves, sunken chest—he was able to make us all think that his was the body of perfection. Today, every bodybuilder who competes in international competition is bigger than Arnold ever was at his peak, and that includes many of the women competitors who are stunning in their muscular development. Enormous bodybuilding competitors twice Arnold's size still express their admiration and respect for the man they acknowledge as the best ever.

Along the way to building and refining his body Arnold also competed, though less extensively, in powerlifting, connecting bodybuilding with titles that would have him dubbed the strongest man in the world. Recognizing weightlifting as an integral component in a physical fitness regimen, Arnold has, more than any other athlete or health figure, influenced an entire nation's attitudes toward fitness and physical improvement. He did this when his own rise to fame was "documented" in the movie *Pumping Iron* in 1977, but he continued to influence these ideas once he got appointed chairman of the President's Council on Physical Fitness and Sports in 1990.

He has been a clever self-promoter, selling his image, his products, his restaurants, and his ideas. Early on in his life in the United States, he began selling nutritional supplements and bodybuilding advice featuring his photograph and bearing the label "Arnold Strong." The products earned him some of the money he needed to begin acquiring real estate and other businesses. Later he leant his name to the Planet Hollywood restaurant franchise but wisely pulled out before he lost money in the unprofitable chain. Never one to let a less-than-successful venture deter him, some years later Arnold opened an Austrian-themed restaurant in Santa Monica, Schatzi on Main, that even featured German-language tapes piped into the bathroom audio systems!

Arnold Schwarzenegger once dominated movie box offices around the United States and overseas. Even when his movies did relatively poorly in the theaters in the United States—often costing more than they earned in this country—an intensive marketing campaign ensured that those same films became international hits. In addition, video and DVD sales of his movies often more than made up for box office failures at home. Arnold's movies had such widespread appeal that he was named the 1985 International Star of the Year by the National Association of Theatre Owners. He has been one of the highest paid movie actors of all time, earning around $30 million for his latest pictures, and for many years he was considered one of the most powerful people in Hollywood.

WHAT'S IN A NAME?

How did someone named Arnold Alois Schwarzenegger get to be one of the biggest men in the world, in more ways than one? All of Arnold's biographers are quick to point out that Schwarzenegger means "black ploughman" as if that indicates something about Arnold's past or future. However, what is more significant about Arnold's name is how much difficulty people have had pronouncing it—and how the mispronunciations have come to be part of the folklore around Arnold. Even in Europe, at the 1966 Mr. Universe competition in England, nobody, according to competitor Rick Wayne, "had yet learned to pronounce his name."[2] Such a tongue-twisting name could have been a barrier to his success in America, but instead it became a household word that was endlessly punned and revised in comical and critical ways.

Movie reviewer Joel Siegel, on the morning television program "Good Morning America," said during his review of *Total Recall* in June 1990, "Who would have thought one of the biggest international box-office stars of the '90s would be named Arnold? Accountants are named Arnold. And Schwarzenegger?" It was a surprise for Hollywood, which tends to favor romanticized or short and memorable, nonethnic names for its stars. Marilyn Monroe started out as Norma Jean Baker. Demi Moore was born Demetria Gene Guynes, and Alan Alda started life with the name Alphonso Joseph D'Abruzzo. Snoop Dog's original name was Cordazer Calvin Boradus, and the debonair Cary Grant was born Archibald Leach. But Arnold Schwarzenegger has (almost!) always been Arnold Schwarzenegger.

Arnold has often recounted how, as he tried to develop a Hollywood career, people would make fun of his name and try to get him to change it. At one point he did try a new name, calling himself Arnold Strong for the movie *Hercules in New York* in 1970 and using the name to sell his bodybuilding food supplements. But he switched back to Arnold Schwarzenegger and began his history-making journey to Hollywood fame and fortune. When he was running for governor of California, the name again became a topic of conversation and humor with late night comedian David Letterman saying, "President Bush has been silent on Schwarzenegger. Of course, he can't *pronounce* Schwarzenegger."

After Arnold became a star, his name provided another kind of fun: coming up with nicknames for the man with the unpronounceable name. The variety of these nicknames also gives an indication of just how widespread Schwarzenegger's influence is. Calling him "Ah-nuld," imitating his Austrian accent, was quite common, even appearing on the cover of TIME before the California recall election on August 18, 2003 as "Ahhnold!?" Other nicknames, not only for Arnold himself, but also for the movie characters so difficult to separate from the actor who played them, showed up in comedy routines, on televised news and entertainment coverage, in jokes, and in straightforward newspaper reporting: Term-Eliminator, Presidator, Mr. Schwarzen-Schnitzel, Mr. Muscle, His Oakness, The Gropinator, Governor Hollywood, The Determinator, Conan the Republican, The Californiator, Abdominal Showman, Android Schwarzenegger, The Austrian Oak, Benedict Arnold, Arnie-bolic Steroids, Arnold Schwarzenazi, Schwarzenheimer, Arnold Schwarzenhammer, and First Colossus.

Political cartoonist Garry Trudeau made a version of his Doonesbury strip after the California recall election that featured a giant talking hand called "Herr Gropenfuhrer." The hand held press conferences but ignored all questions about his behavior toward women. Movie reviews themselves feature nicknames indicating not only a wry view of the films, but of the particular characters Arnold was playing. His role in the movie *Junior*, in which he played a man who becomes pregnant, was renamed, on a Web site allowing only a four-word review, The Materni-nator, Conan the

Ovarian, Full-terminator, Schwarzen-pregger, and The Self-inseminator.[3] How does Arnold feel about the scores of both flattering and potentially insulting nicknames? Just fine, actually: "People have always given me funny nicknames. I really enjoy them a lot."[4]

Whatever one's opinion of the man, there is no denying that he has left his mark on the planet. As a result of all his life's activities, Arnold Schwarzenegger has gained one of the most recognizable faces in the world. He joins a select group of icons who have achieved such recognition—a handful of people whose faces are not only universally familiar, but have become more or less universally understood symbols. Albert Einstein comes to mind, his crazy white hair now a general sign of the brilliant but eccentric scientist. Marilyn Monroe is like that, with images of her standing in for sensuality and flawed love. Sigmund Freud's face has come to be a universal symbol of psychotherapy. Adolph Hitler was not only a real man, but also still is a symbol of virulent prejudice and hatred, political oppression, and the violation of all sorts of human rights. There are very few others that have achieved this kind of notoriety.

RENAISSANCE MAN

How did Arnold get to the same stage of recognition as Einstein, Monroe, Hitler, Sigmund Freud and, perhaps, the Mona Lisa? Perhaps it is because Arnold Schwarzenegger seems to be America's quintessential Renaissance Man, developing expertise in nearly everything he attempts. A Renaissance Man, or *homo universalis* ("universal person") is someone known to be skillful or to excel in a broad range of intellectual fields. It may seem silly to say this about someone who has been generally known as an action figure in violent movies or as an overdeveloped body that flexed for money. But it truly is the case that a look at Arnold is a study of how the world works and how it has taken shape in the twentieth and twenty-first centuries. Now, that's a pretty big claim to make, but if we consider at least ten specific accomplishments, in no particular order, it's a claim easily justified.

- First, Arnold found a niche that could feed mass curiosity—building his body to such an extreme as to awaken wonder, revulsion, attraction, and speculation in his audiences.
- Second, he set about mass-marketing this new product called Arnold Schwarzenegger.
- Third, he learned quickly how to "psych out" the competition. It was no secret that bodybuilder competitors felt intimidated by Schwarzenegger's dominance in the sport.

- Fourth, Arnold made America his home. While one can be a global icon from nearly anywhere in the world, America offered Arnold opportunities for growth that were not available elsewhere. It provided a climate of entrepreneurship, heady competition, and the promise of limitless success.
- Fifth, Arnold diversified—economically, socially, and professionally. He began to network with Hollywood moguls, real estate tycoons, corporate investors, political leaders. His marriage to Maria Shriver may constitute one of his most powerfully American acts—merging political party affiliations, publicity machinery, and family priorities.
- Sixth, Arnold got more and more deeply involved in socially celebrated causes: he became active in raising the national consciousness on fitness, health, and the benefits of sports; he took an active role in Special Olympics and in California's after school programs.
- Seventh, he transformed his own gargantuan successes as a bodybuilder and power-lifter into a nationally recognized annual bodybuilding and fitness convention, the Arnold Classic, in Columbus, Ohio. Through this means, even after his retirement from bodybuilding, Arnold capitalized on his knowledge and experience by creating a venue through which he could remain in the bodybuilding spotlight and continue to collect revenue.
- Eighth, Arnold made sure to own a "piece of the rock"; or, more accurately, a lot of pieces of the rock called the United States. Arnold's keen interest in purchasing American real estate has been part of the foundation of his economic empire.
- Ninth, Arnold turned his vast energies and driving discipline to movies and acting and made himself into one of the most profitable actors in history. Often commanding salaries between $10 million and $30 million per picture, Arnold's movies have grossed, worldwide, nearly $4 *billion* dollars.
- And tenth, but decidedly not last, Arnold Schwarzenegger took the oath of U.S. citizenship, thereby opening the next set of doors: American political office.

What mattered to America was that Arnold provided an idealized image of a true hero, one who could overcome virtually any obstacle, triumph in the face of any adversity, and grow larger with each and every victory. We are always looking for useful heroes in our culture. Comic book heroes have been famous for being super-powerful, for dressing in strange and wonderful costumes, for having bodies that were more flexible, more muscular, more gigantic than ordinary people. Movie heroes have been strong, grounded, rebellious, bold, physically, psychologically, even technologically superior. Cultural heroes have generally been those who have found ways of effecting positive change for society—for children, for the economy, for communities, for the well-being of the citizenry. For millions of people in the United States and throughout the world, Arnold Schwarzenegger, in all his many images, roles, and public rhetoric, seemed to possess many of these characteristics. It never seemed to matter that much of his heroism—at least in those earlier days—was to be found almost exclusively in his movie characters.

Along the way Schwarzenegger has accumulated enormous wealth. Based on the Financial Disclosure Report he filed in 2003 to comply with California's clean government laws, Arnold's net worth is likely far in excess of $100 million.[5] Indeed, some have suggested that this figure is closer to $800 million. Schwarzenegger has investments in an entertainment conglomerate (Oak Productions) from which, in 2001, he drew a salary of more than $22 million. He also has an extensive portfolio that includes holdings in real estate companies, venture capital funds, blue-chip stocks, a charter airline, and of course residuals for all of his movies, product tie-ins, and endorsements He has achieved worldwide fame, numerous prestigious awards and honors, and is husband to a glamorous and politically connected wife and father to their four children. Schwarzenegger maintains contacts with the famous and the powerful throughout the world, and he has both the admiration and the scorn of millions of people in hundreds of cultures across the globe.

We shouldn't, however, think of Arnold Schwarzenegger's life as simply that of a driven man who, on his own, made himself important and famous through hard work and savvy decisions. Every life, but especially big, famous ones, can be seen as part of a larger set of circumstances, dependent on past events, paths set in place by others known and unknown, and larger historical trends that are not of the individual's doing. If we miss the significant webs of connection to history, philosophy, religion, and art that have made an Arnold Schwarzenegger possible, we would miss the bigger picture that helps make sense of his improbable rise to such heights of fame and fortune. Arnold may want us to think, as he has publicly stated many times, that he did it all on his own, but a critical look at the world, past and present, tells us otherwise.

A WONDROUS JOURNEY

It may seem odd to do so, but if we are going to examine Arnold Schwarzenegger's life, we are going to have to take a strange and wondrous journey through time, from the ancient Greeks and Romans to the Crusades in the Middle Ages, from World War II in the 1930s and 1940s to the post-war recovery of Europe and eventually to the entrance of China into today's free market economy. This exploration will involve connections to American political history through the Founding Fathers in revolutionary America, to a beloved assassinated president, a disreputable Republican leader or two, many of the major political icons of the twentieth and twenty-first centuries, and a historic gubernatorial election that will be studied for years in classrooms across the nation. We'll need to make brief visits to the Enlightenment in Europe, the voyages of Puritans and Pilgrims to the New World, the American Revolution, and the treasured documents of the United States: the Declaration of Independence and the U.S. Constitution. For a guy who is mostly known for bulging muscles and violent action films, this is heady company.

In a sense, Arnold Schwarzenegger's story is like an action movie, filled with love, intrigue, ambition, scheming, violence and adventure, some of it real, some of it on the screen, and some of it hard to distinguish. It shows how money is made on a large scale, how politics can be used for both personal gain and the greater good, and how individuals can stand out from among their fellow citizens to have a true and lasting effect on their country and the world. Whether by design and skill or by accidents of fate and luck, Arnold has connected himself to what is considered important and influential in politics, history, economics, and even mythology.

A look at Arnold's life is an exercise in experiencing disbelief that one man could do so much with so little and a hard cold look at just how business, politics, and entertainment mix in America to open doors to the ambitious but close them to the less endowed. It addresses how this nation thinks, talks, dresses, acts, believes, and dreams. It takes in and reflects upon the values of a nation that has presented itself to the world as the only place where a man like Arnold Schwarzenegger can become what his desires and dreams seemed to demand.

Now that he is governor of California, the most populous state in the nation, the third largest state by area and the sixth biggest economy in the world, Arnold Schwarzenegger has an ever-expanding stage on which to present himself, his life, and his ideas. In California he is in the news every day because a governor is always an appropriate focus of attention for state affairs. It is the kind of publicity that any movie star of lesser rank would envy. He no longer has to make Hollywood products and deals to get publicity; his work as governor gets scrutinized every hour of every day, but the public's critical eye on his every move has not always diminished his showmanship and great skills at convincing people that Arnold's way is the only way. One magazine writer, trying to get a handle on Arnold's overall allure as long ago as 1990, thought that, despite his odd name and unique body, Arnold was the epitome of the modern hero. Arnold represented, she said, "pure will, pure power unfettered by memory of a past."[6]

For a cultural icon who sees himself as the epitome of the American Dream, it is the perfect moment. It is the chance to both confirm the dream for himself and to share its facets with a wary post–9/11 nation. The story of Arnold Schwarzenegger has long been presented as the classic tale of the American Dream, the fulfillment of a promise made by the Founding Fathers of this nation that this was the land of freedom and opportunity. Arnold embraced the American dream when he came to the United States in 1968 and has stated repeatedly that he is proof that the dream exists and that it works to motivate people.

Many subjects of biography can be held at arm's length and studied like specimens in a laboratory, analyzed and probed until they reveal the way they work and how they came to be. Arnold Schwarzenegger, however, is such a dynamic and continuously morphing figure that it is sometimes hard to pin him down in this way. This makes a story of his life absolutely intriguing because it presents itself almost as a mythological tale populated with fantastic deeds, larger-than-life actors, earth shattering events, heartfelt beliefs, and challenges to traditional ways of doing things. It is a story that is being told, in part, by the press, by critics, by Arnold's own legacy of movie characters, by his wife Maria Shriver, and especially by Arnold himself as he has marketed himself on television talk-shows, in shopping-mall speeches, press conferences, and sound bytes designed to curry favor with his public. It is the story of both an individual man and the country whose history and values have helped make him one of our most important icons. It is the story of Arnold Schwarzenegger: The American Dream.

TIMELINE: EVENTS IN THE LIFE OF ARNOLD SCHWARZENEGGER

1945   October 20—Gustav Schwarzenegger married Aurelia Jadrny.
1947   July 30—Arnold Schwarzenegger born in Thal, Austria to Gustav and Aurelia Schwarzenegger.
1953   Arnold's father, Gustav, takes Arnold to Graz to see former Olympic swimmer Johnny Weismuller, who is there to dedicate the opening of a new swimming pool. Arnold decides to become a great athlete when he grows up.
1960   Arnold picks up his first bar-bell and decides to be the greatest bodybuilder.
1961   Arnold meets the former Mr. Austria, Kurt Marnul, who invites Arnold to train at a gym in Graz, Austria.
1963   Arnold is runner up at the Steirer Hof Competition, Graz, Austria.
1964   Arnold wins Junior Mr. Austria.
       Arnold places 3rd in Mr. Austria.
1965   Arnold joins the Austrian army. Gustav helps Arnold obtain post as a tank driver (even though he is technically too young for that assignment).
       Later that year, he goes AWOL to compete in the Mr. Europe Junior competition.
       Arnold wins Junior Mr. Europe, Germany.
       Arnold wins Mr. Styria title.
       Arnold wins Austrian Junior Weightlifting Championship.
1966   Arnold completes Army service and returns to Thal.
       Arnold wins the International Power Lifting Championship.

Arnold moves to Munich, Germany, and does his first public body-building exhibition that year.

Arnold wins Mr. Europe competition and is called the 'best built man' in Europe.

Arnold competes in his first amateur NABBA Mr. Universe competition (2nd place).

1967   Arnold buys Putzinger's Gym.

Arnold meets his boyhood idol, former Mr. Universe Reg Park.

Arnold wins the NABBA Amateur Mr. Universe competition.

1968   Arnold wins the German Power-lifting Championship.

Arnold wins his first NABBA professional European Mr. Universe competition. He is recognized as the strongest man in Germany.

Arnold wins the IFBB Mr. International, Tijuana, Mexico.

Arnold arrives in the United States. He places second in his first American Mr. Universe competition. In the same year, he started his own mail-order business (selling, among other things, body-building dietary supplements).

Joe Wieder "discovers" Arnold and agrees to sponsor him.

1969   Arnold wins the IFBB (New York) Mr. Universe title.

Arnold places 2nd in IFBB Mr. Olympia competition in New York (Sergio Olivia wins).

Arnold wins NABBA Mr. Universe (Professional) competition, London, England.

Arnold wins IFBB Mr. Europe (Professional), Germany.

Arnold's friend and fellow body-builder Franco Columbu joins Arnold to tour and train in Venice.

1970   Arnold competes against Reg Park in the Mr. Universe competition and wins.

Arnold meets Jim Lorimer.

Arnold wins his first IFBB Mr. Olympia title.

Arnold wins AAU Pro Mr. World title, Columbus, Ohio.

Arnold plays Hercules in his first movie, *Hercules in New York* (he uses the stage name of Arnold Strong).

1971   Arnold wins his second Mr. Olympia title, Paris, France.

Arnold's brother, Meinhard, dies after a car accident. Arnold does not attend the funeral.

1972   Arnold appears on the television program, *The Dating Game*.

Arnold wins his third Mr. Olympia title in Essen, Germany, this time with his father, Gustav, watching.

Later that year, Gustav Schwarzenegger dies. Arnold does not attend the funeral.

1973   Arnold wins his fourth Mr. Olympia title in New York.
        Arnold plays a hood in the movie, *The Long Goodbye*.

1974   Arnold is cast as a good guy bodybuilder in *Stay Hungry*. He
        begins to take acting lessons. He wins his fifth Mr. Olympia title
        in New York and considers retirement from bodybuilding.
        Arnold is cast as himself in the movie *Pumping Iron*. The book
        by the same title is published that year. Although *The New York
        Times* refused at first to review a book the editors felt would
        have only limited appeal, two months later, *Pumping Iron* was on
        The New York Times bestseller list.
        Arnold appears on television on *The Merv Griffin Show*.
        Arnold appears on the television show, *The Dating Game*.
        Arnold appears on television as Rico in the Lucile Ball TV
        movie, *Happy Anniversary and Goodbye*.

1975   Arnold appears several times on television shows including one
        with Lucille Ball.
        Arnold wins his 6th Mr. Olympia title in Pretoria, South Africa,
        and announces his retirement from professional bodybuilding.

1976   Arnold plays Joe Santo in movie, *Stay Hungry* opens to
        surprisingly positive reviews.
        Arnold is photographed nude by Francesco Scavullo for
        Cosmopolitan magazine.
        Arnold poses with Frank Zane and Ed Corney during a live
        exhibition at the Whitney Museum of American Art. The exhibit is
        called "Articulate Muscle: the Body as Art." The exhibit was de-
        signed to raise funds for post-production publicity for *Pumping Iron*.

1977   *Pumping Iron* opens.
        Arnold writes a best selling book, *Arnold Schwarzenegger: The
        Education of a Body Builder* (with Douglas Kent Hall).
        Arnold plays another bad guy bodybuilder on television. The
        same year, he poses nude for Cosmopolitan magazine.
        For his performance in *Stay Hungry*, Arnold wins a Golden
        Globe award for "Best Newcomer."
        In July, 1977, Arnold meets Sue Moray at Venice Beach; he
        continues a relationship with her until August, 1978.
        Arnold meets Maria Shriver. After dating for a while, Maria
        invites Arnold to the Kennedy family compound in Hyannis
        Port, Cape Cod. There, he meets the Shrivers and Senator
        Ted Kennedy. Eunice Shriver introduces Arnold to the Special
        Olympics, which she founded. Soon after, Arnold becomes the
        Honorary Weightlifting Coach for the Special Olympics.

Arnold signs a contract with Paramount Studios to make the Conan movies.

Arnold attends his first Cannes Film Festival.

Arnold poses, with Dolly Parton, for photographer Annie Liebowitz.

Arnold is painted by Jamie Wyeth.

Arnold appears as Josef Schmidt in the episode, "Dead Lift" on the TV series *The Streets of San Francisco*.

Arnold appears as a muscleman in the episode, "Lifting Is My Life" on the TV series, *The San Pedro Beach Bums*.

1979   Arnold graduates from the University of Wisconsin Superior with a B.A. in Business and International Economics.

Arnold plays Handsome Stranger in the movie, *The Villain*.

1980   Arnold comes out of retirement to earn his 7th Mr. Olympia title in Sydney, Australia.

Arnold appears as Micky Hargitay in the TV movie *The Jayne Mansfield Story*.

1982   Arnold plays Conan in *Conan the Barbarian*.

1983   Arnold becomes a U.S. Citizen.

1984   *Conan the Barbarian* out-earns every other movie

Arnold plays Conan again in *Conan the Destroyer*.

Arnold plays The Terminator in *The Terminator*.

1985   Arnold proposes to Maria Shriver.

Arnold is voted NATO International Star of the Year.

Arnold plays Kalidor in the movie, *Red Sonja*.

Arnold plays John Matrix in the movie *Commando*.

October, Arnolds is the cover story in *People* magazine ("Maria Shriver's Man Arnold: Why JFK's niece loves the savviest, silliest strongman in showbiz")

1986   Arnold and Maria marry.

Arnold plays Mark Kaminsky (aka Joseph P. Brenner) in the movie, *Raw Deal*.

1987   Arnold plays Major Alan "Dutch" Schaeffer in the movie, *Predator*.

Arnold plays Ben Richards in the movie, *The Running Man*.

Arnold is awarded a star on the Walk of Fame.

1988   Arnold plays Capt. Ivan Danko in the movie, *Red Heat*.

Arnold plays Julius Benedict in the movie, *Twins*.

1989   The first Planet Hollywood opens.

The Arnold Classic is born.

Katherine Schwarzenegger is born.

1990   Arnold becomes Chair of the Inner City Games, Los Angeles, CA.
Arnold is appointed Chairman of President's Council on
Physical Fitness and Sports.
Arnold plays Douglas Quaid/Hauser in the movie, *Total Recall*.
Arnold has his first directing job in an episode of *Tales from the
Crypt*.
Arnold plays Det. John Kimble in the movie, *Kindergarten
Cop*.
Arnold directs episode ("The Switch") of the TV series, *Tales
from the Crypt* and also appears at the beginning of the show.
Arnold is appointed Grand Marshall of the 59th Hollywood
Christmas Parade.

1991   Arnold plays The Terminator again in *Terminator 2: Judgment
Day*.
Maria Shriver gives birth to the second Schwarzenegger baby:
Christina.
Arnold is awarded a Humanitarian Award from Simon
Wiesenthal in Los Angeles.

1992   Arnold completes 50 state tour for the President's Council.
Arnold directs made-for-TV movie, *Christmas in Connecticut*
(he also plays Man in chair in front of Media Truck—uncredited).
Arnold opens a restaurant, Schatzi on Main.

1993   Arnold is named "International Box Office Star of the Decade"
by NATO ShoWest.
Arnold plays Jack Slater/Himself in *Last Action Hero* (Arnold is
also Executive Producer).
Arnold accepts chairmanship of CA Governor's Council on
Physical Fitness.
The Third Schwarzenegger is child born: Patrick.

1994   With Maria by his side, Arnold's hands, feet, and signature are
immortalized at Mann's Chinese Theater.
Arnold plays Harry Tasker in the movie *True Lies*.
Arnold plays Dr. Alex Hesse in the movie, *Junior Opens*.

1995   Arnold teams up again with James Cameron for production of
T2:3D.

1996   *T2: 3D: Battle Across Time* (short) Opens at Universal Studios, FL.
Arnold receives an Honorary Degree of Humane Letters from
Univ. of Wisconsin Superior.
Arnold plays Howard Langston in the movie, *Jingle All the Way*.
Arnold plays U.S. Marshal John "the Eraser" Kruger in the
movie, *Eraser*.

1997   Arnold is awarded Leadership Award by Simon Wiesenthal
Center.

Arnold plays Mr. Freeze/Dr. Victor Fries in the movie, *Batman
and Robin*.

Arnold and Maria have a fourth child, Christopher.

On April 16, Arnold undergoes elective heart surgery to repair
faulty valve.

1998   Arnold wins the Moving Picture Ball's American Cinema-
theque Award.

Arnold's mother, Aurelia, passes away (she has a heart attack
upon visiting the gravesite of Gustav).

1999   Arnold plays Jericho Cane in the movie, *End of Days*.

T2:3D opens at Universal Studios, Hollywood.

Arnold is honored with Ring of Honor by hometown of Graz,
Austria.

2000   Arnold makes trip to China for Special Olympics.

Arnold receives Muhammed Ali Humanitarian Award (presented to him by Ali).

Arnold auctions off his Hummer to benefit Inner City Games.

Arnold signs to star in *T3*.

Arnold is awarded Father Flanagan Service to Youth award.

Arnold plays Adam Gibson in the movie, *The 6ᵗʰ Day*, which
opens at the Tokyo Film Festival, then premiers in the United
States (Arnold is also Producer).

2001   Arnold is honored at the World Sports Awards with "Lifetime
Achievement Award."

AFMA names Arnold "Box Office Champion."

Arnold helps launch the Hummer H2 in New York.

Arnold travels to South Africa for Special Olympics.

Arnold is honored with Taurus Honorary Award.

Imadec University in Vienna awards Arnold an Honorary
Doctorate in Business Administration for his Life
Achievements.

Arnold plays White Wolf (voice) (uncredited) in movie,
Dr. Dolittle 2.

Arnold appears in the TV broadcast, 2001 *Winter Special
Olympics*.

2002   Arnold plays Gordy Brewer in the movie, *Collateral Damage*,
which opens #1 at the box office.

Arnold plays Baron von Steuben (voice) in TV series *Liberty's
Kids: Est. 1776*.

Arnold submits 750,000 signatures for the After School Education and Safety Act (Proposition 49).

T3 begins production.

Proposition 49 passes.

Arnold receives honorary degree, Doctor of Humane Letters at Chapman University.

25th Anniversary of *Pumping Iron* premiers on Cinemax.

2003   August 7—Arnold announces his candidacy for California governor on the *Tonight Show* with Jay Leno.

October 7—Arnold is elected Governor of California in the California recall election.

November 17—Arnold is sworn in as Governor.

Arnold plays the Terminator in *T3: the Rise of the Machines*.

Arnold plays a bar patron (uncredited) in the movie, *The Rundown*.

2004   Arnold plays Prince Hapi in *Around the World in 80 Days*.

2005   Arnold plays Jack Slater in the video, *AC/DC: Family Jewels*.

Arnold plays himself in *The Kid & I*.

2006   Arnold rejects and returns Ring of Honor after politicians in his hometown of Graz, Austria are critical of Schwarzenegger's tacit approval of capital punishment. He also demands that Schwarzenegger Stadium no longer use his name.[7]

NOTES

1. Rick Wayne, *Muscle Wars: the Behind the Scenes Story of Competitive Bodybuilding* (New York: St. Martin's Press, 1985), p.83.

2. Ibid., p. 59.

3. See http://www.fwfr.com/display.asp?ID = 2384.

4. Jill Lawrence, "Schwarzenegger won't shy away from confrontation," *USA Today*, June 9, 2005. Accessed July 26, 2006, http://www.usatoday.com/news/nation/2005-06-09-schwarzenegger-cover_x.htm.

5. Lance Williams, "Schwarzenegger worth $100 million, experts say," *San Francisco Chronicle*, August 17, 2003, p A18.

6. Suzanne Moore, "Brand Loyalty," *New Statesman and Society*, August 3, 1990, p. 38.

7. Chronology sources: http://www.schwarzenegger.com, www.IMDb.com, www.musclememory.com, www.bodybuildbid.com.

Chapter 1

AMERICAN DREAM ARNOLD

Before we get even deeper into the details of Arnold's life, to his evolution from a skinny, sickly Austrian boy in post–World War II Europe to a body that impressed the world, from a poor and humble beginning to enormous fame and wealth, it's worth considering just what ideas drove this unbelievable journey to international stardom and political power.

People have been trying to figure Arnold out for years. An unauthorized biography of Arnold written by Wendy Leigh in 1990[1] claimed that the motivation for his ambition and drive was not just a vague desire to improve his lot in life or to be happy. The motivation was supposedly psychological, caused by the fact that in his childhood Arnold had a violent and drunken father who he feared, a mother who could not give him the attention he needed, and an older brother who was healthier, more handsome, more athletic, favored by his parents, and destined for great things. In this view, Arnold's strict upbringing and fear of failure would drive him well into adulthood to do things that would not only bring him tremendous success, but also prove that he was his own man now, making decisions and taking on challenges that, in the least, would have annoyed his father and shocked his mother.

Even if these claims were true, even if all of his success is simply due to a desire to compensate for a bad beginning, it is not something that is any longer a part of the story Arnold has built about himself. Somehow, someplace along the way, Arnold grabbed hold of a set of goals, interests and desires that he used to explain himself. He gave it the historically loaded and somewhat unfortunate name of "The Master Plan." Later, he switched his explanation, saying that he was trying to reach the American Dream.

THE MASTER PLAN

In business or community development, a master plan is an overall comprehensive picture of how to meet a set of goals. It is a set of ideas, procedures, and expectations that have an ultimate goal that should be met within a specific period of time. Many businesses and institutions make master plans for 3 years or 5 years to track their progress. Organizations with multiple buildings like colleges, museums, zoos, businesses and amusement parks develop master plans to coordinate future building and renovations. It has become a common term for this type of activity.

But the choice of calling his life's ambitions "The Master Plan" can be a bit shocking for those who are familiar with the history of Nazi Germany and the use of that term to describe their scheme for world domination in the 1930s and 1940s. It is even more surprising given Arnold's background. Arnold's father Gustav joined the National Socialist party in Austria in 1939, right after Adolph Hitler annexed Austria in a nonviolent takeover during a series of actions that led to World War II. Heinrich Himmler was the man in charge of Adolph Hitler's defense squadron, the Schutzstaffel or SS, which made up a large part of the National Socialist German Workers Party, also known as the Nazi Party.

Himmler, one of the most powerful and influential men in Adolph Hitler's Third Reich (the empire Nazi Germany was trying to reclaim), developed a set of ideas and goals that helped guide Hitler's plan for Germany. Himmler was interested in restoring the glory of pure-blooded Germans and in establishing idealistic agricultural communities for young, fertile Nordic families who would go back to the traditional ways of the land and create a pure race. Himmler used ideas from mythology, German folk life, and archaeology to justify defining Germans as the master race qualified to rule the world. As author Heather Pringle explains in her book, *The Master Plan*,[2] Himmler carried out Hitler's objectives, including the extermination of all undesirables, without question. He was the architect of the Final Solution, which was designed to eliminate Jews completely. His overall vision for the future of Nazi Germany was his Master Plan.

So the term "Master Plan" is a bit weighed down by a history from the part of the world Arnold was born into. Nevertheless, he used the term freely to describe his plan for his life. The Master Plan that Arnold designed for his life was described in detail in a book of photographs published by Arnold's friend George Butler.[3] Butler also wrote and co-directed *Pumping Iron*, the 1977 quasi-documentary film that made Arnold famous. The photographs in the book have also become famous, showing Arnold in the 1970s training and posing during his bodybuilding career.

Butler recalled a recurring dream that Arnold had been having in 1972. Arnold was living with his girlfriend, Barbara, and taking classes at night school. In his dream, he was "king of all the earth and everyone looked up to him."[4] According to Butler, 1972 was also the year in which Arnold described his "Master Plan," which he was already fully involved in implementing for himself. The plan entailed these elements: Arnold would go to America, become the greatest bodybuilder that ever lived, educate himself with the necessary skills for achieving his goals, learn to speak English, make a lot of money, invest his money in real estate, work in the movies as an actor, producer and director, become a millionaire, get rid of anything from his old life that stood in his way, get invited to the White House, marry a glamorous and intelligent woman and become involved with politics.[5]

BORN FOR THE USA

The timeline of Arnold's life shows just how successful he was in carrying out these steps in a timely manner. But more remarkable than his rapid achievement of these goals was the fact that he was able to accomplish all of these things in spite of the fact that he came to this country with little more than ambition and a vision. That is what makes people who don't even like his movies admire him as a person; that is what makes him an American icon and a symbol of what Americans can be if they try hard enough. It reveals a man of limitless ambition and a vast appetite for success and, as he himself has said, a man who is not at all modest about his achievements.

Arnold stated in Butler's book that ever since the age of ten, he felt he had been born in the wrong country. He wanted to be the best at something, and Austria could not offer what he needed. From early on, the Master Plan was tied to the idea of coming to America. In an interview with writer Studs Terkel in a book titled, *American Dreams: Lost and Found*, Arnold stated that when he was 10 years old he dreamed of being an American. "I felt it was where I belonged," he said.[6] Coming to America meant that Arnold's Master Plan could eventually be repackaged as the achievement of the American Dream. Arnold's story now could be a more general one shared by people everywhere who thought about a better life and how to achieve it.

Arnold today, in very public and dramatic ways, claims to be the best representative of the promise of the American Dream that has ever existed. The story Arnold tells of his life focuses on what he did to get out of Austria and how he was able to carry out the American Dream. It is worthwhile, then, to trace the history of this idea of the American Dream and why it has gripped not only immigrants like Arnold Schwarzenegger who made it work, but those who still struggle to obtain a piece of it.

THE AMERICAN DREAM

Historian Jim Cullen writes that the American Dream can be considered our "national motto," and it has had a hold on our collective imagination for centuries. Yet, the American Dream is not something that can be definitively proven right or wrong. As he explains, "The American Dream would have no drama or mystique if it were a self-evident falsehood or a scientifically demonstrable principle. Ambiguity is the very source of its mythic power."[7] The most "alluring and insidious" form of the American Dream, says Cullen, and the one that is prominent today, is the one associated with Hollywood. The Hollywood version promotes fame and fortune achieved with little effort.

The American Dream is a concept that goes back to the founding of the nation and even before to the arrival of the early European settlers to the British colonies. Remember that the people who came to the New World of North America were trying to get away from conditions in the Old World, Europe. The earliest settlers were convinced of the corruption of the religions and the governments of Europe that were dominated by church-state alliances and by governments that were inherited rather than elected. They had a firm belief, whatever the differences between the various groups that sailed to America, that things could be different and better. This became the basis of a set of beliefs, religious and secular, that came to form the American Dream.

America seemed to offer a new beginning for these earliest settlers as much as it did for Arnold Schwarzenegger: the possibility of owning land, of working in new and interesting ways, of forgetting the oppressions of the past, of learning a new language and taking on a new identity. Many more and different immigrants came to American after the first settlements by mostly religious groups in the seventeenth century. By the middle of the eighteenth century, the many inhabitants of the thirteen British colonies saw that although they seemed to have developed religious freedoms in these new lands, their economic interests were not being served by the leaders in Great Britain, who were extracting revenues from the colonies to pay for debts in Europe.

Maybe even more important than these economic woes were the new ideas taking hold intellectually around the western world. Beginning around the middle of the seventeenth century and extending through the eighteenth century and beyond, the traditional hierarchies and religious authority were no longer the sole basis for making decisions in society. In this period, known as the Enlightenment, relations between the individual and the state were being called into question. Governments were being rethought as a contract between the state and the individual rather than as an imposed order from above by the ruling traditional families.

In the thirteen British colonies, these ideas and a series of confrontations developed into the American Revolution, which asserted the rights of the colonies to decide their own future. Battles were fought between the colonists (not yet Americans at this point) and the British forces. By 1776, the colonists were ready to make a Declaration of Independence, and in it we see the formal proposal that America was a place based on an idealized state of being that was found nowhere else. With the Declaration of Independence, the founding fathers confirmed the proverbial "city on a hill" idea of America that they told the early settlers would be a model for the rest of the world, the place where the American Dream could actually be seen and carried out.

THE TWO DREAMS

One of Arnold Schwarzenegger's political role models was Ronald Reagan, former Governor of California (1967–1975) and President of the United States (1981–1989). Reagan often referred to aspects of the American Dream throughout his political career. When he used the "city on the hill" concept in his farewell speech to the nation in 1989, he was continuing his long commitment to keeping the American Dream alive as the major myth of the nation. In that speech he said:

> I've spoken of the shining city all my political life, but I don't know if I ever quite communicated what I saw when I said it. But in my mind it was a tall proud city built on rocks stronger than oceans, wind-swept, God-blessed, and teeming with people of all kinds living in harmony and peace, a city with free ports that hummed with commerce and creativity, and if there had to be city walls, the walls had doors and the doors were open to anyone with the will and the heart to get here. That's how I saw it and see it still.[8]

Reagan always seamlessly combined these two aspects of the American Dream: the economic and the moral. In his remarks at the Republican

National Convention in 1988 he stated, "We were unashamed in believing that this dream was driven by a community of shared values of family, work, neighborhood, peace, and freedom" when talking about the moral aspect and, "The dream we shared was to reclaim our government, to transform it from one that was consuming our prosperity into one that would get out of the way of those who created prosperity," when talking about the economic aspects, all in the same paragraph.[9] In a radio address to the nation in 1986, he stated, "Here in America we've been fortunate to be the keeper and custodian of a dream—a dream that began this nation, a dream that millions of people hope to share in someday."[10]

From Reagan's attention to the American Dream, Arnold learned his place as a participant in that collective goal. In an article he wrote for USA Today after Reagan's death in 2004, Arnold told how Reagan inspired him:

> He used to talk about the letter he received from a man who said, "You can go and live in Turkey, but you can't become Turkish. You can go and live in Japan, but you can't become Japanese. You can go to live in Germany or France, but you can't become German or French." But the man said that anyone from any corner of the world could come to America and become an American.
>
> When I heard President Reagan tell that story, I said to myself, "Arnold, you Austrian immigrant, he is talking to you. He is saying that you will fit in here. You will be a real American, able to follow your dreams."[11]

These two aspects of the American Dream were clearly defined by scholar Walter R. Fisher as the "materialistic myth of individual success" and the "moralistic myth of brotherhood."[12] The materialistic aspect of the myth encouraged freedom to "do as one pleases" and to use hard work, focused effort, self-reliance, and initiative to bring about individual mobility and economic security. From the beginning of the thirteen colonies, this sort of rugged individualism was a necessity for surviving in the New World. Later, as the western territories of the continent were made available for exploitation, the materialistic aspect of individual success drove many Americans westward. Today, Arnold offers himself as a model of a focused and determined effort that everyone should share.

The moralistic aspect of the American Dream can also trace its roots to the early settlers and later to the American revolutionaries. The Declaration of Independence's statement that "all men are created equal" has been considered for generations as the core of the American Dream's moral message even if it actually left large segments of the population out of the equation for decades. In 1787, when the U.S. Constitution was ratified, and in the several years later when the Bill of Rights were adopted, the inequalities of the original declaration were still not addressed, but the idea of the American Dream prospered.

The idea of working together to make that city on the hill a reality for everyone, however, has been both a goal for the culture as a whole and an often-forgotten aspect of the national motto. The two forms of the American Dream can still be found in American culture. The individual economic form, however, has become prominent, and there is little question that Arnold Schwarzenegger has become one of its best examples.

The concept of having and fulfilling a dream of material abundance—dream homes, dream vacations, a dream job—dominate American advertising. This shift can also be illustrated by the widespread participation in mega-lotteries and other kinds of gambling that promise instant wealth not by the traditions of hard work over time, but by instant rewards through luck. Television game shows, which have always rewarded small parts of the American dream like a new appliance or a car, now provide winners with the whole thing: "Who Wants to Be a Millionaire" rewards enough cash, and "American Idol" provides both money and fame.

Actually, coming to America was a necessary component of making the dream come true and not acting on it was not the American way. Arnold stated boldly in his 1977 autobiography that he knew he was destined for greatness but not if he stayed in Europe.[13] He was just 30 years old when he wrote his biography, and he had achieved many of the goals he had set for himself when he left Europe. Arnold first articulated his life goals when he was very young. In his autobiography he explains that at one point when he was 15, his friends convinced him that religion (he was brought up a Catholic) was silly because if you wanted something, you had to obtain it yourself, not ask God for it. Arnold learned with his bodybuilding that he, and no one else, was in control of how his life developed and what he did with it. His beliefs sound just like those of the early American colonists.

His first goals for himself came as a result of seeing pictures of bodybuilder Reg Park. He read about Park in bodybuilding magazines and built his training routine based on Parks successful program, the one that had made him a world champion. He also saw Park in the movies, playing Hercules roles and showing off his massive body. Park's example gave him the goal: he wanted to be big, a big guy, massive, a real man, "the biggest, most powerful person in bodybuilding."[14] In 1991, Arnold told

Muscle & Fitness magazine, "I did not want anything about my life to be little. What I wanted was to be part of the big dreamers, the big skyscrapers, the big money, the big action. Everything in the United States was big. That's what I enjoy about this country. And there's no monkey business; I mean, you have to make an effort to be little here."[15]

All the other things would follow from making his body big. But to do any of this, he had to leave Austria and Germany and travel to the land where dreams can come true, to America. When, years later, he had achieved the final component of his own version of the American Dream, being elected to political office, Arnold was invited to address the Republican National Convention in New York in 2004. After joking that, "What a greeting! This is like winning an Oscar! ... As if I would know!" Arnold began a speech in which he defined himself as the ultimate American. For Arnold, his simple life story as a poor immigrant who made it big in American was a model for his fellow citizens:

> My fellow Americans, this is an amazing moment for me. To think that a once-scrawny boy from Austria could grow up to become Governor of California and stand in Madison Square Garden to speak on behalf of the President of the United States. That is an immigrant's dream. It is the American dream.[16]

It was a long, arduous, fascinating journey for Arnold, traveling from a home in a small medieval town in Austria to the land of big dreams and great successes. But just what made that "scrawny boy" take on such a journey and how did he succeed in becoming the best example of the American Dream?

NOTES

1 Wendy Leigh, *Arnold: An Unauthorized Biography* (Chicago: Congdon & Weed, Inc., 1990).

2. Heather Pringle, *The Master Plan: Himmler's Scholars and the Holocaust* (New York: Hyperion, 2006)

3 George Butler, *Arnold Schwarzenegger: A Portrait* (New York: Simon & Schuster, 1990).

4. Ibid., p. 21.

5. Ibid., p. 22.

6. Studs Terkel, *American Dreams: Lost and Found* (New York: Ballantine Books, 1980), p. 141.

7. Jim Cullen, *The American Dream: A Short History of an Idea That Shaped a Nation*, (New York: Oxford University Press, 2003), p. 7.

8. Ronald Reagan's farewell speech to the nation in 1989: http://www.reaganlibrary.com/reagan/speeches/speech.asp?spid=21.

9. Reagan's remarks at the Republican National Convention in 1988: http://www.reagan.utexas.edu/archives/speeches/1988/081588b.htm.

10. Reagan's radio address to the nation in 1986: http://www.reagan.utexas.edu/archives/speeches/1986/51786a.htm.

11. Arnold Schwarzenegger, Editorial, *USA Today*, June 8, 2004: http://www.usatoday.com/news/opinion/editorials/2004–06–08-arnold_x.htm.

12. Walter R. Fisher, "Reaffirmation and Subversion of the American Dream." *Quarterly Journal of Speech*, vol. 59 (1973). 160–67.

13. Arnold Schwarzenegger and Douglas Kent Hall, *Arnold: The Education of a Bodybuilder* (New York: Simon & Schuster, 1977).

14. Ibid., p. 17.

15. Julian Schmidt, "Arnold," *Muscle & Fitness* (August 1991): 91.

16. Schwarzenegger's speech at the Republican National Convention in New York in August, 2004: http://www.cbsnews.com/stories/2004/08/31/politics/main639869.shtml.

Chapter 2

AUSTRIAN ARNOLD

One of Arnold's many biographers, George Butler, once referred to Arnold Schwarzenegger as a "Mountain, Himself, with an ego that was slightly bigger than the Austrian Alps...."[1] No matter how rich, famous, or powerful—or American—that Arnold has become, it is impossible to talk about his life's most significant moments without taking into account his country of birth.

Tucked neatly in the center of Europe, touched on its borders by Germany, Switzerland, Slovakia, Czech Republic, Italy, Hungary, Slovenia, Croatia, and Liechtenstein, Austria is a relatively small country of 32,000 square miles. Just a little bit smaller than the state of Maine, Austria's population of approximately 8 million is around 6.5 times that of Maine's. When you consider that nearly two-thirds of Austria is covered in mountains, you begin to realize just how richly populated Austria's biggest cities are.

Six months of military service is compulsory for men in Austria, but women are not permitted to serve in the army in any capacity. Education is compulsory up to the age of 15. There are 12 universities, all free, catering to 200,000 students. Austria is considered by many travelers to be a wonderful place to visit and explore (especially if you like coffee! On average, one Austrian drinks 55 gallons of coffee a year![2]), and Austria's history is rich. Tourist books on Austria often use the German word *gemütlich* to describe this country. Roughly translated, *gemütlich* means "warm and congenial." But it wasn't always so genial a place.

FROM ANSCHLUSS TO THE PRESENT DAY

On March 11, 1938, the Nazis marched into Austria. Already torn by war and sagging in spirit, Austrian forces offered virtually no resistance. In April 1938, a referendum was held that seemed to support the *Anschluss* or annexation. Austria was incorporated into Hitler's Third Reich. During World War II, Austria was part of the Nazi war machine. After the war, it suffered the same fate as Germany, divided into four zones by the victorious Allied powers (Russia, France, Britain, and the United States). In 1955, independence was restored subject to a pledge of eternal neutrality. This pledge on October 26, 1955, celebrated now as National Day, was the birth of the Democratic Republic of Austria. Eleven years later, in 1966, all foreign-occupying forces finally left the country. On January 1, 1995, having shed a great deal of its past reputation as a puppet of fascism, Austria joined the European Union.

There are five major cities in Austria: Innsbruck, Linz, Salzburg, Vienna, and Graz—the city closest to Arnold Schwarzenegger's birthplace. Graz is the second largest Austrian city, with a population of about 240,000 (about twice that of Topeka, Kansas), and is the capital of Styria, a county in the southeast corner of Austria. Nestled in between scenic hills, to the north, east and west, Graz "opens" only to the south. The first settlements date back to 800 A.D. and through the medieval times, its Styrian landowners took over the town and turned it into a flourishing trading center. With natural protection on three sides, Graz has always been an important strategic location.

When Adolph Hitler rode into Graz, he was greeted with such enthusiasm by the Styrians that he bestowed upon the city the honorary title: die Stadt der Erhebung ("the town of elevation"). It should be noted that the Grazian enthusiasm was not a product of anti-Semitic fervor but, rather, a reflection of the hope that the Third Reich's annexation of Austria would mean new prosperity for the economically depressed Styrians. The fact that Hitler was a fellow Austrian only served to make him seem even more charismatic. In a remark from her unauthorized biography of Arnold, Wendy Leigh notes that "Arnold reportedly confided to his girlfriend Sue Moray that when his mother saw Adolph Hitler, she almost swooned."[3]

ARNOLD'S FAMILY

Arnold's Grandparents, Karl Schwarzenegger and Cecilia Hinterleitner

Not a lot has been said about Arnold's paternal grandfather, Karl Schwarzenegger. He died young in an accident, but while alive, he'd been large and strong. His wife, Cecilia, lived to the age of 80, and the two had four children: Franz, Alois (from whom Arnold gets his middle name), Gustav, and Cilly.[4] Like his father, Gustav Schwarzenegger became a metal worker for a while before joining the Austrian army as a teenager. Some say the elaborate uniform of the Austrian military was particularly appealing to the attention-loving Gustav.

Arnold's Mother, Aurelia Schwarzenegger

Arnold's mother, Aurelia Jadrny, had married Gustav when she was 23. Widowed already, Aurelia warmed to the attentions of the 38-year-old Gustav, whom she married in 1945. Aurelia was primarily a housewife, though she occasionally worked in the kitchen at the Café-Restaurant Thalersee near their home in Thal. She reportedly became a very traditional and subservient spouse. She gave in to Gustav's demands—including his forbidding her to wear pants (a new fashion at the time).[5] Her duties were confined mainly to the chores of maintaining the household—cooking, cleaning, washing, sewing—and, of course, ensuring that her husband was well-fed and his clothing was properly cleaned and pressed.

With her two boys, Meinhard and Arnold, Aurelia seemed to be a democratic parent, almost to the extreme: she even felt strongly that her nearly same-aged sons should be the same height. Toward that end, according to one biographer, "If one boy grew taller than the other, she gave the other more food to eat."[6]

Arnold's Father, Gustav Schwarzenegger

Born on August 17, 1907, Arnold's father, Gustav Schwarzenegger was a very large, often fierce man. A talented musician who could play six different instruments, especially the flugelhorn,[7] Gustav was also a strict taskmaster, who believed strongly in discipline, obedience, and hardship as an ideal shaper of character. Demanding perfection from his two sons, he, himself, was far from perfect. A heavy drinker, prone to bursts of violent temper, and a rather unsympathetic parent, Gustav was a complex man who expected his boys to be top athletes, to appreciate classical music and museums, and to maintain a heavy work-load in school and at home.

Around seven years before marrying and starting his family, Gustav made a decision that would have a ripple effect far into the future: he joined the National Socialist German Workers Party, known as the Nazis, on July 4, 1938.[8] In the 1930s, it was common for Austrians to see in Adolph Hitler a champion of order and discipline and to welcome his brand of social control. But only very small numbers of Austrians actually became members of the Nazi Party. It is important to note that until Germany annexed Austria in March of 1938, it was illegal in Austria to be a Nazi party member. Gustav joined the party just a few short months after it became legal to do so. Although already a police officer, Gustav's decision to join the Nazi party meant he would have to meet the condition of being of pure Aryan blood.

The Aryans were a mythical Nordic race of earlier Europeans who provided a model for Hitler's renewed Germany. The idea that there was a "race" or lineage of people who were tall, slim, and muscular with blonde hair and blue eyes and that they represented the perfect humans who lived in Europe in a previous age did not originate with the Nazis, however.[9] The concept was concocted from several notions about the origin of the German people. First, there was an idea that the people of Europe originally came from India because of similarities found in the vocabularies of languages found in the two places. The earliest immigrants from India were supposedly mystical warriors and priests drawn to the mountains of Europe. German nationalists of the nineteenth century later decided that instead of India being the origin of Germany, it was the north of Europe, the Nordic countries, that provided the early settlers. The Germans ended up believing in this Nordic perfection which connected a particular appearance with characteristics like "boldness, a natural aptitude for great undertakings, self-reliance, sound judgment, a love of justice, a deep well of energy and creativity" as well as a "talent for warfare."[10]

Gustav apparently had no difficulty in meeting the Aryan ideal, and the Nazi party welcomed him into its ranks. In 1939, Gustav volunteered for a special military group known as the *Sturmabteilungen*, or "storm troopers." After being wounded, he retired from the military in 1943. After World War II, the Allies investigated hundreds of Nazi officers and their war-crimes, but there was no significant investigation into Gustav Schwarzenegger's Nazi activities. Gustav's record was sufficiently clear for him to resume his work as a police officer and, later, Police Chief of Thal.

Gustav met his future wife while she was working in a "wartime office dispensing food stamps."[11] Aurelia Jadrny was impressed by the tall officer, and the two were married in October of 1945. Gustav was 38 years old, the same age his son Arnold would be when he got married.

Some say Gustav's heavy drinking was a result of his war-wounds.[12] He had taken some shrapnel in his legs during World War II. It has also been speculated by one of Arnold's biographers that alcohol was a means for Gustav to forget his past involvement in the Nazi Party. Gustav's drinking continued throughout the 1940s and 1950s. Between his excesses and his temper, his tiny staff of men were intimidated by him. Gustav's frustrations may also have been related to financial problems: his salary was comparatively small—the equivalent of around $250 per month[13]—and his expenses had grown immediately after getting married when his two sons were born within almost exactly a year of each other.

Whatever his reasons for doing so, after beginning his work day with a late-morning snack, it has been reported that Gustav would begin drinking. Sometimes, at night, he would drink so much, he had to be carried home.[14] These same drunken episodes often led Gustav to rant and rave about Aurelia's behavior, her alleged indiscretions and her supposed flirtations with other men. The fact that Gustav was significantly older than his young wife may have been one factor in his jealous outbursts. He was extremely possessive of Aurelia—"Reli" as he would call her—and his possessiveness even provoked him to demand that she cover her arms completely, even in hot weather, when they attended church.[15]

Arnold's Brother, Meinhard Schwarzenegger

Meinhard, a strong and sturdy boy, was born on July 17, 1946, one year and 13 days before his brother Arnold. Whereas Arnold was frequently sick as a child, Meinhard was a healthy, sturdy youth. He was clearly the favorite son of Gustav—a favoritism that would have dramatic effects throughout the boys' childhoods. According to one biographer, Gustav so preferred Meinhard over Arnold that he frequently sent Arnold to stay with his Uncle Alois in Murzzuschlag. It should be noted that even Aurelia seemed to have a special feeling for her older son, "calling him by the affectionate nickname Meinhardl."[16]

As one writer put it, Meinhard "was the school bully, tormenting those weaker and smaller."[17] More significantly for the young Arnold, Meinhard represented one more force to be reckoned with on the home front. Modeled, perhaps, on the bullying the boys faced at the hands of their own father, they developed an aggressive edge that would characterize their relationship not only to each other, but to others around them. As the favored and more physically gifted boy, Meinhard generally came out on top of the sibling rivalry. It was a contest to try to win Gustav's approval. Gustav, for his part, would set the two boys up in competition with one another, announcing each time, "Let's see who's the best!"[18] More often than not, it was Meinhard who would out-run, out-fight, out-ski, even out-study his younger brother.

The two boys developed into young delinquents, often terrorizing others. When the boys would be reported, their Police Chief father—never one to withhold punishment for household infractions—rarely disciplined them for their more public transgressions. One thing led to another, and Meinhard ended up being expelled from the Marschall School and sent to reform school. He had become a bully in the image of his father but with even fewer of the social graces. Arnold, too, had taken to bullying the village children, and like Meinhard, these actions were rarely if ever punished by Gustav. One villager said, in retrospect, "That is why the Schwarzeneggers were hated in Thal. Today everyone loves them, but forty years ago no one wanted to have anything to do with them."[19]

When Meinhard was a young man, he left Thal and went to Germany. A lover of women, Meinhard found that women were very much attracted to him as well. Among his many girlfriends, one of them, Erika Knapp, had a son, Patrick, with him in 1968. Whereas Arnold's success earned him Gustav's affection at last, Meinhard had slipped from Gustav's favor. He started to drink. He began working for a publisher in Kitzbühel, rented one room of someone else's house, and kept on drinking heavily. At one point, Meinhard assaulted a woman and went to prison. While his brother Arnold had already gone to America and was on his way to a stellar career, Meinhard was sliding backward into oblivion.

On the evening of May 20, 1971, a drunk Meinhard Schwarzenegger was killed in a car accident. "Deep down I always expected something to happen to him," Arnold has said of his brother, although he did not attend his funeral, just as he would be absent from his father's funeral a year and a half later. "He lived on the edge more than I ... Now, I wish he was here to enjoy all this with me. Back then, I just brushed it off."[20] In many ways, Meinhard's life, and death, served as reminders to Arnold that failure to work hard and persevere could lead to an unsatisfying life and the death of everything Arnold was now striving to achieve.

ARNOLD'S BOYHOOD

On July 30, 1947, little Arnold Schwarzenegger was born into something of a crowd. Austria was a defeated country, having been part of a despicable alliance with Nazi Germany whose downfall was also Austria's. The tiny nation of Austria was occupied by three very large forces: the Russians, the Americans, and the British, who now controlled this southeastern region of Austria, including Graz. Already surrounded by mountains to the north, east, and west, Graz now counted among its everyday population soldiers from three powerful nations.

Arnold and his family lived upstairs in a house owned by an Austrian nobleman. The house, several hundred years old, was also a tight fit, and like many of the local houses, it had no indoor plumbing and was badly in need of general repairs. "We had no flushing toilet in the house. No refrigerator. No television. What we did have was food rations—and British tanks around to give us kids an occasional lift to the elementary school."[21] What they did not have were many of the modern conveniences that we now take for granted; the entire village of Thal had to share just three telephones, and there was just a single television in the town.[22] Thal also had no doctor, which meant that Aurelia had to nurse the often-sick Arnold back to health.

Between Gustav's drunken rages and Meinhard's bullying, Arnold had all he could do to keep a cool head and develop an independent spirit of his own. But he certainly did. As one writer put it, "Arnold knew a secret magic that would help his dreams come true. The magic that Arnold used is simple: he worked very, very hard."[23] He also knew, in his heart, that he was destined for something big, beyond Austria. Buried in his imagination was an idea that America was the place for him. He told photographer/ biographer George Butler, "I admire America because it is a powerful country. I admire its economic system, its freedom, and its money. It is a rich country. Its people are open-minded. But I didn't understand all this when I was ten years old. There was something else. A subconscious drive to come here."[24]

But Arnold didn't always just work hard. He had a rich fantasy life as well. Partly in reaction to his father Gustav's insistence on a love of the fine arts, and partly as a more ordinary kind of early adolescent escapism, Arnold turned away from music, art, and high culture and turned toward a dream of becoming big, strong, and dominant. One biographer identifies a larger-than-life comic book muscleman hero, "Sieguard," who caught young Arnold's attention. But soon his tastes for heroes progressed to action stars of the movie screen. Arnold would sneak into theaters and absorb stars like John Wayne, Tarzan-portrayer and swimming star Johnny Weismuller, and, most significantly, the Hercules films that starred Steve Reeves and South African muscleman Reg Park.[25] It was the latter who would be indelibly fixed in Arnold's imagination as the image of muscular development and power.

Never particularly good at schoolwork, Arnold was, nevertheless, an attentive learner when it came to human nature. Like everyone else in

Thal, Arnold kept up with the village talk and paid attention to things around him. By the time he finished the eighth grade, while something of a trouble-maker like his brother, Arnold was gravitating toward a career in carpentry with less and less interest in academics. But when he happened to notice a magazine featuring a photograph of Reg Park, famed South African bodybuilder and movie star, and the man Arnold loved to watch in the movies, the die was cast for Arnold's future. "Everything I dreamed of was embodied in Reg Park," Arnold said.[26] The dream was, in some sense, a simple one: to become a superman.

Arnold had already begun working out with weights and calisthenics. While on the school soccer team at age 15, his coach decided that his players would benefit from lifting weights. When he went for his first visit to the gym and saw, for the first time, a group of powerful weightlifters, he knew he'd found something special. "[T]here it was before me—my life, the answer I'd been seeking. It clicked."[27]

While his brother excelled at team sports, Arnold found himself more and more drawn to athletic endeavors that emphasized individual achievement, and weightlifting, as a start, fit the bill perfectly. Perhaps one motivating factor was Arnold's desire to emerge from Meinhard's shadow and from the controlling influences of Gustav. "Maybe I was competitive with my brother or trying to prove something to my father."[28] But it is equally true that Arnold took great satisfaction in realizing that he was very good at building his own physical strength and his physique. It was an athletic process for which he had to rely on no one but himself. As he put it, "by the time I was thirteen team sports no longer satisfied me. I was already off on an individual trip."[29]

There was at least one other reason that the young Arnold took so readily to weightlifting and bodybuilding, something that would become a theme throughout his life. "These weight lifters were my new heroes. I was in awe of them, of their size, of the control they had over their bodies."[30] Control over his body, control over himself, control over his destiny—as a young teen, Arnold already had come to understand something about himself that would be his dominant motivation throughout his life.

Those early days of training really helped to define Arnold's character. In his autobiography, Arnold recounts his very first serious gym workout in this way:

> I rode my bike to the gym, which was eight miles from the village where I lived. I used barbells, dumbbells, and machines. The guys warned me that I'd get sore, but it didn't seem to be having any effect. I thought I must be beyond that. Then, after

the workout, I started riding home and fell off my bike. I was so weak I couldn't make my hands hold on. I had no feeling in my legs: they were like noodles. I was numb, my whole body buzzing. I pushed the bike for a while, leaning on it. Half a mile farther, I tried to ride it home again, fell off again, and then just pushed it the rest of the way home. This was my first experience with weight training and I was crazy for it.[31]

For a lot of us, feeling so stiff and sore that we couldn't even lift a comb the next morning might discourage us from further trips to the gym. But Arnold was different. "It was the first time I'd ever felt every one of my muscles ... I learned that this pain meant progress."[32]

ARNOLD'S EARLY TEEN YEARS

As a young teen of 14 and 15 years old, Arnold had already determined that he would one day leave Thal and head for the "big city" of Graz, a few miles away, and then beyond. Images of his fantastic hero, Reg Park, and of his own future as a superman came to dominate his thoughts. As the son of a domineering, competitive, and at times ferocious man, Arnold had absorbed and distilled a great deal of what he'd experienced as a young child. He already had developed the kind of determination that would, throughout his life, be characterized as unstoppable. It was this quality of commitment to his goals that distinguished Arnold not only from so many others against whom he would compete later in life, it also ultimately separated his vision of a future from that of his brother's.

In 1952, when Arnold was just 5 years old, another Austrian, Kurt Marnul began a bodybuilding career. In those days, bodybuilding was hardly the phenomenon it would become a decade and a half later. Marnul was a fitness expert whose emphasis on heavy weightlifting helped him to become Mr. Austria. In 1958, Marnul created the Athletic Union Graz (or Graz Athletic Union) located "in the bowels of Graz's Liebenauer Stadium."[33] The Athletic Union was the place for Austria's bodybuilding elite to train, and Arnold, like so many Austrians, knew about Mr. Austria. But unlike many Austrians, Arnold was determined not only to know about Marnul, but to meet him and to draw from his knowledge in his quest to become great. And there was at least one other reason Arnold was drawn to Mr. Austria: the Austrian bodybuilding champion was a lady's man who "tooled around Graz in a sports car with a voluptuous blonde by his side."[34] For Arnold, who was himself starting to notice the opposite sex, the attraction that women felt for men with big, powerful bodies was yet another big incentive for him to become the biggest.

In 1961, Arnold got his chance to meet Kurt Marnul, who saw in Arnold a "tall but thin" young man. Indeed, Marnul thought more of brother Meinhard's chances for bodybuilding greatness. "Meinhard looked much more like a potential bodybuilder"," Marnul has remarked.[35] But Meinhard had none of Arnold's raw determination and sense of discipline. It was Arnold who grabbed the opportunity to train at the Athletic Union with Marnul and the other heavy-lifting men. "The first day Arnold trained," Marnul recalls, he said, "I will be Mr. Universe."

Arnold trained every single day for hours each day. It was an obsession with him, and after just a few years, he had gained around 25 pounds of muscle from his workouts. The gym was supposed to be closed on Sundays, but Arnold found ways of breaking in by forcing open a window. It meant a lot to him to be able to get in his daily three or four hour lifting routine.[36] "I loved the feel of the cold iron and steel warming to my touch and the sounds and smells of the gym."[37] There was something especially significant about Arnold's decision to devote himself to these workouts. According to biographer Laurence Leamer, Arnold "realized that joining the Athletic Union was the first decision he had ever made on his own."[38]

Arnold made another momentous decision at that time, and like so many of his early decisions, this one would have long-range consequences. At the routine suggestion of Marnul, Arnold accepted the first of many doses of anabolic steroids to aid him in his quest for muscular superiority. Ingesting substances for athletic or strength advantages was not a new idea. The ancient Greek wrestlers, for example, would consume enormous quantities of rare—or raw—red meat to build up fighting muscles. In the 1930s, a team of scientists, primarily in Germany, began developing and experimenting with ways to create a synthetic form of testosterone (a male hormone) to help treat men who were unable to produce enough testosterone for normal growth, development, and sexual functioning. During World War II, scientists discovered that this artificial form of testosterone could actually help malnourished soldiers gain weight and improve performance.

After the war, this same artificial hormone found its way into the world of sports. Athletes from Europe and Russia found that the use of steroids enhanced their performance, increased their strength, and gave them a competitive edge previously unattainable. After 1956, an American doctor, John Zeigler, began developing an even more refined version of this artificial hormone, what we now know as anabolic steroids.

Zeigler's steroid was so effective that for the next decade and a half, steroids were widely used not only by Olympic athletes but also by professional sports players, even those in high school. It was not until 1975 that the International Olympic Committee (the IOC) banned the use of anabolic steroids in Olympic competition. After that, sports and athletic organizations around the world began to limit the use of steroids or to ban them altogether.[39]

Back in the 1950s and 1960s, then, it is not difficult to imagine that bodybuilders were powerfully attracted to these steroids. In the 1960s, there was nothing illegal about using anabolic steroids, though it was generally accepted "wisdom" that otherwise healthy adults should not take them. But there was nothing "normal" about the world of bodybuilding, and when Marnul introduced the 15-year old Arnold to the steroids that all the other bodybuilders were using, it was simply par for the course—a necessary ingredient in the recipe for greatness.

Stories vary on the quantity of steroids Arnold was taking as a young teenager. One biographer reports that "the injections began almost immediately after Arnold started training as a body-builder" and that a fellow bodybuilder claimed that, "Arnold took steroids in doses that terrified the other bodybuilders."[40] Another biographer points out that such out-of-control steroid use was unlikely, that it "was hardly his standard approach to anything involving his chosen sport."[41] What most of the stories about Arnold's early career claim is that by age 15, Arnold was a regular bodybuilder at Marnul's gym and a regular user of anabolic steroids.

While Arnold's newfound passion may not have completely changed him from his own bullying ways, the weightlifting workouts left him little energy for too much foolishness. Increasingly, he drifted away from Meinhard's influence and allied himself with his new group of bodybuilder friends. He still pursued his apprenticeship as a carpenter, but now even that activity was made to fit into his larger plans. On the job, he'd volunteer to pick up heavy loads of lumber as a way to bring weight training into his job. After work, in the evening, he'd forego all offers to play pick-up games of soccer and ride his bicycle to the gym in Graz to workout for hours.

One would think that Arnold's new focus might be seen as a positive step for the young teen. But his parents were not happy with his obsession, and his mother Aurelia was concerned that his use of steroids was dangerous. "When I discovered what he was doing, I was concerned that it might be harmful to him."[42]

Arnold's father refused to allow Arnold to work out every day at the gym, but Arnold got around this restriction by putting together his own gym in the basement of his house. Year round, in the heat of summer and the bitter cold of winter in the unheated basement, Arnold would supplement his gym workouts with these at-home training sessions. In Arnold's mind, he could hear his new mentor, Kurt Marnul, telling him, "Go on until you cry out. That is the secret of the biggest bodybuilders. They train beyond the barrier."[43] As a very young teen, Arnold was determined not only to train beyond the barrier, but to shatter it.

ARNOLD THE TEENAGER

It has been suggested that Arnold's life—particularly his early years—follows the trail blazed by heroes in the Horatio Alger stories of the nineteenth century. Alger's stories heroicized the young "city boys" who started life in poverty in a big American city like New York or Philadelphia. With a combination of remarkable courage and moral strength, these boys would overcome all sorts of adversity to achieve greatness and, to varying degrees, wealth. One element these stories often shared was that the protagonist would encounter an older man of means, who would shepherd him through many of life's hazards and who would provide guidance, wisdom, and social connections.

For Arnold, Kurt Marnul was perhaps his first such mentor—an older man who took a lively interest in Arnold's potential as an athlete and took him under his wing. Another such mentor was the father of one of Arnold's new friends and training partners: Karl Gerstl. Gerstl was a medical student who also had a passion for bodybuilding, and despite the 13-year difference in age, the two became friends. Karl's father, Alfred Gerstl, took a deep liking to young Arnold, and Arnold became a frequent houseguest in the Gerstl home. It is worth mentioning, in light of his Arnold's father's wartime history, that the members of Arnold's newfound surrogate family were Jewish.

The Athletic Union gym became, for Arnold, the place to meet a number of these kinds of mentors, each offering Arnold a different set of teachings. Arnold explained, "Each of them became a father image for me. I listened less to my own father."[44] In addition to Karl Marnul and Karl Gerstl, Arnold found in Helmut Knaur, a man more than 35 years his senior, another kind of role model. It was Knaur who "cured" Arnold of going to Catholic Church each Sunday with his family. He "gave me a book called *Pfaffenspiegel*,[45] which was about priests, their lives, how horrible they were, and how they'd altered the history of the religion."[46] Arnold promptly told his family that he would no longer be attending church, that it was a waste of his time. While this did not particularly upset his father, it didn't sit well with his mother.

Arnold also listened less and less to his old friends, most of whom "thought I was crazy." Arnold didn't care, and he knew, already, that his goals were profoundly different from theirs. "My drive was unusual, I talked differently than my friends; I was hungrier for success than anyone I knew."[47] It was a remarkable bit of self-knowledge for a 15-year-old boy.

While Arnold may have found his scholastic studies to be dull, his love of everything bodybuilding had a surprising side effect: "I had resisted memorizing anatomy in school; now I was eager to know it. Around the gym my new friends spoke of biceps, triceps, latissimus dorsi, trapezius, obliques."[48] Arnold's sudden interest in anatomy was followed by a growing interest in human psychology. The youthful Dr. Karl Gerstl, himself an avid weight-trainer, provided just the right blend of increased knowledge of the body and of the way the human psyche works. It was Dr. Gerstl who was able to explain to Arnold why he sometimes felt held back from training his hardest and how to overcome such occasions. "It's not your body, Arnold ... It's in your mind. On some days your goals are just clearer. On the bad days you need someone to help get you going ... You just need some prodding, some challenge."[49] Karl, himself, frequently supplied that prodding, provoking Arnold to train harder, sometimes by initiating contests to see who could do the greatest number of lifts that day.

Everything Arnold was doing in those days was designed to make him grow larger. This would become perhaps the single-most important theme of his life. In his early days at the gym, he developed a vision of his ideal-ized body: "I wanted to be a big guy ... I dreamed of big deltoids, big pecs, big thighs, big calves; I wanted every muscle to explode and be huge. I dreamed about being gigantic."[50] Soon, as his training regimen became more and more intense, Arnold saw that his work was producing big results. "My mind was into looking huge, into being awesome and power-ful. I saw it working. My muscles began bursting all over. And I knew I was on my way."[51]

Toward what was Arnold on his way? The list is very, very long! But at that time, as a teenager, Arnold was mainly on his way to a few very specific things: groundbreaking muscular development, a heightened sense of purpose, both physically and psychologically, and a relatively new relationship to members of the opposite sex.

ARNOLD ON THE VERGE OF MANHOOD

One of the discoveries Arnold made as his body began to grow and change was that girls were reacting to his appearance. "There was a certain number of girls who were knocked out by it and a certain number who found it repulsive."[52] It didn't much matter to Arnold how they felt, as long as they felt something. To him, any overt reactions renewed his desire to stand out more and more. "I wanted to get bigger so I could really impress the girls who liked it,"[53] Arnold noted in his autobiography, but equally intriguing to Arnold were the girls who found his huge muscles revolting. He saw his muscular growth as a way to unnerve those girls who found him hard to look at. Attention was attention, and in the bodybuilding world, attention was also everything.

It was time to start applying all he had learned, all he had taught himself, and all the hunger he had for bodybuilding mastery. In 1964, at the age of 16, Arnold entered, and won, the Junior Mr. Austria contest. More remarkably, he placed third in the *adult* Mr. Austria portion of the competition. But it was not Arnold's intention to be Mr. Austria, nor even to remain *in* Austria for any longer than he had to. It was time to make the kind of big move that would characterize the rest of Arnold's life. It was time to build a body too large to be contained by his native country.

NOTES

1. George Butler, *Arnold Schwarzenegger: The True Story Behind the Making of a Champion* (New York: Simon & Schuster, 1990), p.13.

2. See http://www.nescafe.co.uk/coffee_people/cup_consumption/index.asp.

3. Wendy Leigh, *Arnold: An Unauthorized Biography* (Chicago: Congdon & Weed, 1990), p. 8.

4. Ibid., p. 7.

5. Ibid., p. 9.

6. Ibid., p. 11.

7. Ibid., p. 7.

8. Ibid., p. 6.

9. Heather Pringle, *The Master Plan: Himmler's Scholars and the Holocaust* (New York: Hyperion, 2006), p. 28.

10. Ibid., p. 36.

11. Leigh, *Arnold*, p. 7.

12. Laurence Leamer, *Fantastic: The Life of Arnold Schwarzenegger* (New York: St. Martin's Press, 2005), p. 17.

13. Leigh, *Arnold*, p. 9.

14. Ibid., p. 9.

15. Ibid., p. 10.

16. Ibid., p. 11.

17. Leamer, *Fantastic*, p.19

18. Leigh, *Arnold*, p. 13.

19. Ibid., p. 17.

20. See John Hotten, "Dying to be Arnie," October 31, 2004, at http://www.ergogenics.org/arn6.html.

21. Nigel Andrews, *True Myths: The Life and Times of Arnold Schwarzenegger* (Seacaucus, NJ: Carol Publishing Group, 1995), p. 15.

22. Susan Zannos, *Arnold Schwarzenegger: A Real-Life Reader Biography* (Bear, Delaware: Mitchell Lane Publishers, 1999), p. 6.

23. Ibid., p. 5.

24. Butler, *Arnold Schwarzenegger*, p. 25.

25. Leigh, *Arnold*, p. 18.

26. Rick Wayne, "Reg Park ... a Hero's Hero." *Muscle Builder/Power* (August/September 1976).

27. Arnold Schwarzenegger and Douglas Kent Hall, *Arnold: The Education of a Bodybuilder* (New York: Simon & Schuster, 1977), p.14.

28. Richard Corliss, "Box-Office Brawn," December 24, 1990, *Time*. Accessed July 26, 2006, http://www.time.com/time/archive/preview/0,10987,972006,00.html.

29. Schwarzenegger and Kent Hall, *Arnold*, p. 14.

30. Ibid., p. 15.

31. Ibid., p. 15.

32. Ibid., p. 16.

33. Leamer, *Fantastic*, p. 25.

34. Ibid., p. 25.

35. Nigel Andrews, "Arnold Starts Building," at The Arnold Fan presents: The Beginning, on http://www.thearnoldfans.com/bodybuilding/history.htm.

36. Ibid.

37. Schwarzenegger and Kent Hall, *Arnold*, p. 15.

38. Leamer, *Fantastic*, p. 25.

39. "Anabolic Steroids," CESAR—Center for Substance Abuse Research, University of Maryland, http://www.cesar.umd.edu/cesar/drugs/steroids.asp.

40. Leigh, *Arnold*, p. 27.

41. Leamer, *Fantastic*, p. 26.

42. Jack Neary. "Arnold: Lover of Life," *Muscle Builder/Power* (June, 1979).

43. Leigh, *Arnold*, p. 27.

44. Schwarzenegger and Kent Hall, *Arnold*, p. 14.

45. Arnold is referring to a book entitled *Der Pfaffenspiegel*. The book was written in the 1840s in Germany. More recently, it has been translated into English as *The Mirror of the Clerics* by German author Otto von Corvin. See Otto von Corvin, *Scandals in the Roman Catholic Church* (Salt Lake City: Merkur Publishing, 2003).

46. Schwarzenegger and Kent Hall, *Arnold*, p. 32.

47. Ibid., p. 17.

48. Ibid., p. 17.

49. Ibid., p. 22.

50. Ibid., p. 17.

51. Ibid., p. 23.

52. Ibid., p. 26.

53. Ibid.

Chapter 3

THE BODY ARNOLD

Arnold Schwarzenegger has built his entire adult career around his physical body. As a bodybuilder, a movie star, a promoter, a salesman, and a politician, Arnold has capitalized on his long-running public image as the man who trained his body to be the biggest and the best. Americans have never known Arnold without his exaggerated anatomy. He represents a kind of solidity and durability that few humans have ever both achieved, never mind sustained, throughout their public lives. For nearly 30 years, Arnold's body has also been the size of movie screens, adding another facet to the sense of bodily grandeur. For almost 40 years, Arnold's body has been working its way through the American imagination, transforming the very idea of what a body can and should be, how it should look, how it is disciplined, and what it can accomplish.

One source of this fascination has always been the *size* of Arnold's body. People have wondered just how big he really was at his prime, and how much of that size and bulk he has retained. There have been rumors throughout his career that he is really much shorter than he says, or much taller than he appears. He is heavier—or lighter—than the reports about him claim. He has been described as "larger than life," and then as "larger than larger than life."[1] The public examination of his body—and his life—prompted someone to describe him as "a gargantuan specimen under the public microscope."[2] His photographer friend George Butler once referred to him as "the Mountain" to which the "Muhammad" of the national media would come.[3]

THE IMPORTANCE OF BEING BIG

In 1991, Arnold gave an interview in Joe Weider's *Muscle & Fitness* magazine and said about his ambitions, "I did not want anything about my life to be little. What I wanted was to be part of the big dreamers, the big skyscrapers, the big money, the big action. Everything in the United States was big. That's what I enjoy about this country."[4] Arnold would not have been able to enjoy this country of bigness if not for the one factor that brought him to global attention: his very large and muscularly perfected body, a body whose size quickly became the stuff of myth. From his first days in the American spotlight, Arnold's body pushed the boundaries of muscular development, bulging in unexpected ways and blowing the minds of audiences throughout the land.

Arnold spent years in sweaty gyms blasting his muscles with stress, pain, and—as he has often admitted—steroids because bodybuilding gave him a passport to bigness and greatness. Every one of his over-sized muscles contributed to his journey from being a nobody in a small village in Austria to becoming the biggest man in the "biggest" country in the entire world.

Why do people participate in an activity like bodybuilding? Some observers have speculated that it demonstrates a need for obsessive self-control, or a desire to hide insecurities about masculinity, or because it gives protection from bullies. But many bodybuilders find pleasure or pride, like Arnold did, in improving themselves and enjoy seeing the results of hard work and focus. Whatever the reasons, a built body gets attention.

Over the years, even before most people were aware of bodybuilding, Arnold expanded our ideas about the limits of what could be done with, and thought about, the body. He learned to use clever tricks of the eye and mind to achieve the appearance of being the biggest and most perfect body. His statements in the "documentary" *Pumping Iron* showed that winning at bodybuilding was about creating the impression of bigness by projecting confidence and by posturing as much as it was about concrete muscle development and physical dimensions.

When posing in a competition, bodybuilders are like magicians who can redirect attention away from their flaws and create the illusion of bodily perfection. Artie Zeller, who photographed hundreds of bodybuilders for magazines, was convinced that Arnold's body "doubled in size" when he flexed.[5] When *Pumping Iron* producer George Butler showed Arnold some photos taken when he was relaxed, Arnold complained, "These photos are not me ... there's no pump. No monster arms. I look tiny."[6]

Arnold has not been "tiny" since he was a toddler. And yet the measurements Arnold claims to have had when he was at the top of his form—Height 6 feet 2 inches, Weight 235 pounds, Biceps 22 inches, Chest 57 inches, Waist 34 inches, Thighs 28.5 inches, Calves 20 inches[7]—are almost "tiny" compared to today's bodybuilding champions. All the bodybuilding champions after Arnold have been virtually monstrous, outweighing him, "out muscling" him, presenting unimaginably gigantic bodies. In terms of bodybuilding, Arnold was no longer the biggest body, even by the time of his last championship win.

Years later the bodybuilding world had changed, and size was redefined. On the cover of the February 2004 issue of *Muscle & Fitness*, Ronnie Coleman, Mr. Olympia for the seventh time, declared, "I am the World's Biggest Man." At 287 pounds, all hard, sculpted muscle and no fat, he is huge. He went on to win the 2005 Mr. Olympia, tying Lee Haney's eight consecutive victories. Arnold's six Mr. Olympias in a row, and seven overall, were starting to seem much less significant. Lee Haney won the Mr. Olympia title eight times, one more than Arnold.

Yet neither Coleman nor Haney ever achieved the kind of bodybuilding star-power that Arnold did. Dorian Yates was the heaviest Mr. Olympia ever, but few outside of bodybuilding's inner-circles have ever heard of him. Lou Ferrigno was the tallest Mr. Olympia at 6 feet 5 inches, and he starred in his own TV series, "The Incredible Hulk," but Ferrigno never enjoyed a fraction of the celebrity that Schwarzenegger commanded.

Even some of today's female bodybuilders, bulked beyond belief, are nearly as big or even bigger than Arnold was in his iron-pumping days. Nicole Bass, often described as the "Largest Woman Bodybuilder in the world today," lists herself at 6 feet 2 inches tall, "230 lbs of muscle," a 50-inch chest, 30-inch waist, 18-inch arms, 28-inch thighs, and 18-inch calves. She can bench press more than 300 pounds.[8] Like most bodybuilding measurement statistics, these are most certainly exaggerated. But what is true is that by today's standards, Arnold Schwarzenegger in his prime would be considered a "small" professional bodybuilder.

Yet, no matter how many years have passed since Arnold was acknowledged as the world's most perfectly developed man and despite the fact that he actually retired from professional bodybuilding more than 25 years ago, people still associate the name Arnold Schwarzenegger with huge muscles, larger-than-life stature, and scores of championships in bodybuilding competitions all over the world. They think of Mr. Universe and Mr. Olympia, biceps pumped, pectorals expanded, calf-muscles flexed, godlike poses, oiled and suntanned skin, and the raw power associated with someone who once devoted his life to lifting enormous amounts of weight while crafting every thick strand of muscle and sinew in his body.

At nearly 60 years of age now, Arnold's body has not been particularly noteworthy for a long time. So how do we explain this persistent national and international image? How do we account for people thinking, along with bodybuilder and author Leslie Heywood, that, "Arnold Schwarzenegger … is considered one of the founding fathers of bodybuilding"[9] when he really was not? To answer questions like this, we have to take a close look not only at Arnold Schwarzenegger's experiences as a bodybuilding champion, but also at the strange and fantastic world of bodybuilding itself.

A LITTLE HISTORY ABOUT BIG MEN

It was not always the case in American culture that a muscular body was considered the best kind of body a man could have. Until the end of the nineteenth century, a muscled body indicated that a man was a laborer, someone whose body showed the evidence of his economic status. Men who worked in offices or who supervised laborers did not develop muscles and visible strength. But as the nineteenth century turned into the twentieth, a concern was developing that American culture was becoming too feminized, and most men were what today Arnold would call "girlie men." So a shift in the culture developed, and "a nationwide health and athletics craze was in full swing, as men compulsively attempted to develop manly physiques as a way of demonstrating that they possessed the virtues of manhood."[10] Bodybuilding became one way to develop and display manhood.

The first famous bodybuilder, Eugen Sandow (born Friedrich Müller in 1867), got his start when Oscar Attila (born Louis Durlacher in 1844), a professional strongman, saw in Sandow a potential protégé. Attila taught Sandow how to re-shape his gymnast's body into a bodybuilder's physique. Attila had a bodybuilding "school" in Brussels, and Sandow became a "student" there, using a shot-loading barbell. This was a long bar with hollow spheres attached to each end. One could fill these globes with lead shot or sand to produce a barbell of various weights. Sandow is widely regarded as the pioneer of bodybuilding, "the man who made the world mad for muscles."[11]

By 1898, Sandow had started a magazine called *Physical Culture* (which later became the famous *Sandow's Magazine of Physical Culture*). He was considered by many to be one of the most famous men in the world. Pictures of Sandow appeared on postcards and advertisements, and in many of these pictures, he had posed wearing only an imitation fig leaf. He was portrayed as Adam-like—as though he'd been carved right out of nature itself. The great showman Florenz Ziegfeld took Sandow on some of his world tours, billing him as "The World's Most Perfectly Developed Man" and "The Strongest Man in the World." Sandow would pose as a "living Greek statue" and then perform feats of strength. Of course, he was not the strongest or most perfectly developed man, but audiences didn't seem to mind that exaggeration. They flocked to see him, and pretty soon, new magazines, exercise equipment, even diets began to grow out of Sandow's notoriety. By the time Sandow died in 1925, he had created a permanent place for himself in the history of bodybuilding as a public and profitable venture.

At around the same time—the end of the nineteenth and beginning of the twentieth centuries—two other men helped to turn bodybuilding into a popular concept among young men. Bernarr Macfadden was a bodybuilder and an entrepreneur who had developed a product he called a "chest-expander." The device was a rubber strap (or spring) connected to two handgrips. One would hold these grips and pull them apart, stretching the band and expanding the chest-muscles. Macfadden also launched a new magazine called *Physical Development* in 1898 as a ready-made way to market his products and his philosophy of fitness and exercise. One of his slogans was: "Weakness is a crime! Don't be a criminal!"

In 1903, Macfadden did something that defined bodybuilding in so powerful a way that it would become the standard for future bodybuilders. That year, he sponsored a special contest at Madison Square Garden in New York. Contestants would show off their physiques, emphasizing, of course, their massively developed chests. This physique contest was the first of its kind, and the poses used by contestants remain, for the most part, the types of poses bodybuilders of today still use. Eighteen years later, in 1921, Macfadden's contest was geared to determine "The Most Perfectly Developed Man in America," and the winner of that competition was a very well known strongman and bodybuilder by the name of Angelo Siciliano. He wasn't well known by *that* name. Instead, he came to be known by his new Americanized marketing name: Charles Atlas.

Supposedly, as a teen, Siciliano had been at the beach on Coney Island, and a bully had kicked sand in his face. From that moment on, went the story, Siciliano was determined to rebuild himself into a strongman who would be intimidated by no one. As Charles Atlas, he began to market a mail order course combining calisthenics and isometrics, with some nutritional and general health advice thrown in. The business was a failure. Then, with the help of promoters, Atlas tried an approach that would become one of the most well-known strength and fitness marketing ploys: he advertised in comic books and renamed his exercise course, "Dynamic Tension." Suddenly, Atlas looked like a genius! In short order, sales were booming, and the buyers were from a population Atlas had not realized would be so passionate about his product. Teenage boys got caught up in the fervor to develop big muscles. "Dynamic Tension" promised boys that they would build bodies that "women will desire and men will envy." In this way, Charles Atlas became one of the early powerbrokers of strength training and, standing behind his slogan, "Nobody picks on a strong man," he became an icon of masculinity as well.

The 1930s and 1940s saw a new development that would help immortalize the image of bodybuilders as sex objects and exhibitionists. In Santa Monica, California, Muscle Beach was *the* spot for bodybuilders to gather—to train in public and to perform acts of strength and a variety of stunts all to the delight of excited crowds on the beach boardwalk. Some of the big shots at Muscle Beach were people whose names would become household words: Jack La Lanne, Joe Gold (founder of Gold's Gym), and John Grimek, who would be voted Mr. America in 1946. (Mr. America competitions originated in 1939 under the auspices of the American Athletic Union, or AAU.) Also flexing his muscles at Muscle Beach was a man named Harold Zinkin, who invented the Universal Gym, for decades the most widely used piece of exercise equipment among bodybuilders and weight-trainers. By the 1950s, Muscle Beach had closed, and the locus of bodybuilding activity moved to Venice Beach.

In the same year that Grimek became AAU's Mr. America, another bodybuilding organization was crafted by a Canadian promoter, Ben Weider. That organization, the International Federation of Bodybuilders (IFBB), became the most widely recognized bodybuilding guild, and by the 1950s, Ben's brother Joe—himself a bodybuilder—had created a major business with various bodybuilding, fitness, and exercise magazines, all promoting what became known as the "Weider philosophy" of training—one that emphasizes the Weider brothers' idea of total fitness and muscularity.

The result of Joe Weider's vast influence on the bodybuilding world was that in 1965, he succeeded in fully professionalizing competitive bodybuilding. He did this by creating and organizing a new competition that would be even more expansive—and of course profitable—than the competitions held by rival organizations. This new bodybuilding venue was the Mr. Olympia contest, sponsored by the Weiders' new IFBB, and participants were poached from the Mr. Universe competition sponsored by the National Amateur Body Builders' Association (NABBA).

One of these NABBA bodybuilders was a fascinating young Austrian bodybuilder with an equally fascinating name: Arnold Schwarzenegger. In Arnold, Joe Weider saw a powerful new addition to the bodybuilding universe and a potential treasure-trove of marketability.

ARNOLD BUILDS A BODY

Bodybuilding's popularity rose, fell, and then leveled out throughout the 1950s. The people who paid attention to it were mainly other body-builders and weight-trainers. But in 1958, bodybuilding re-emerged in popular culture when Hollywood producer Joseph E. Levine released the foreign film, *Hercules,* in the United States. The leading man was a body-builder by the name of Steve Reeves.

Reeves was the personification of the ideal male. Not only was he hand-some, he had the physique that many considered to be perfect. *Hercules* was a smash hit at the box office, and pretty soon Hollywood was regu-larly producing "sword and sandal" epics featuring other notable bodies in leading roles—people like Lou Degni, Gordon Scott, and the man who was Arnold's boyhood idol, Reg Park. But again, the public interest in these movies, and in the musclemen who populated them, began to wane. Bodybuilding just wasn't a major attraction outside of its own limited community.

Enter Arnold Schwarzenegger. When he first appeared on the American scene, Arnold Schwarzenegger seemed to be *all* body, a fleshy billboard for the sport of bodybuilding, but not much else. Unable to speak clear English, he was initially the familiar image of the dumb bodybuilder, all body and no brain. But he changed the face of bodybuilding, not just by lifting it out of its seedy history and making a second-rate sport into an art form, but by putting a much more intelligent, strategic face on it. That strategy began long before he came to America.

THE FOUNDATION

From the moment that Arnold walked into the Graz gym owned by Austrian bodybuilding champion Kurt Marnul, he knew he was home. Everything about the workouts made sense to the 15-year-old. In his auto-biography, he wrote that, "I'm not exactly sure why I chose bodybuilding, except that I loved it. I loved it from the first moment my fingers closed around a barbell and I felt the challenge and exhilaration of hoisting the heavy steel plates above my head."[12]

It would not be an exaggeration to say that Arnold Schwarzenegger began his bodybuilding career at that moment. His parents thought he was crazy because his early training left him stiff and in pain. His mother, Aurelia, could not understand why her son could barely walk the next morning. He couldn't lift his arm to comb his hair, and his hand could not properly grip his cup of coffee. Aurelia was so alarmed, she summoned her husband, Gustav, and said, "Look what he's doing to himself."[13] Gustav was merely amused. Arnold didn't care; no matter how his parents might react, he knew he'd found his calling in life, and he was rabid with desire to get back to training. As he put it, "My drive was unusual … I was hungrier for success than anyone I knew."[14]

Arnold learned early on that well-built, strong men were respected by others and shared advantages others did not have. Men like Steve Reeves could break into the movies and become celebrities. Muscular men ended up on magazine covers. In one such magazine, Arnold saw his first photograph of Reg Park. "I responded immediately to Reg Park's rough, massive look." As usual, Arnold was most attracted to size—to bigness. Park was "an animal," and for Arnold, this was the way he, too, wanted to be seen: as a big man. Arnold burned the image of Reg Park's muscularity and poise into his mind and began a training regimen that would have broken most more experienced weightlifters. He pushed his training program to 6 days a week. Although his father, Gustav, worried about his son's obsession, he could not say much in response to Arnold's vow, "I want to be the best-built man in the world."[15]

Not only did the teenager want to be the best, he already had formulated a plan beyond that. As he told his father, "I want to go to America to be in the movies."[16] This was a moment that would characterize Arnold's entire life: having a plan, aggressively pursuing the necessary steps to get there, and then, along the way, begin formulating the next, even bigger plan. Working out 6 days each week was, for Arnold, just a necessary step to the giant goals he'd already set for himself. According to one biographer, Arnold's father's reaction to his son's American dream was to say, "I think we'd better go to the doctor with this one, he's sick in the head."[17] But if Arnold was "sick" with anything, it was a kind of love-sickness: the love of training hard, of growing his body, and of achieving goals that would lift him from obscurity to fame. The relatively small country of Austria could no longer contain Arnold for much longer. "I'd always had a claustrophobic feeling about Austria. 'I've got to get out of here, ' I kept thinking. 'It's not big enough, it's stifling. ' It wouldn't allow me to expand. There never seemed to be enough space."[18]

Surrounded by pictures of Reg Park that he'd taped to the walls, Arnold lifted and lifted and lifted some more. The goal was to build up a massively muscular body and then "chisel it down to get the quality." According to Arnold, "you work on your body the way a sculptor would work on a piece of clay or wood or steel." Determined to get himself to 250 pounds of muscle, Arnold kept adding more and more weight to the barbells and dumbbells, "blasting" his muscles until they began "busting out all over."[19]

One of the things Arnold noticed right away was that becoming very big also meant, for him, gaining enormous confidence. When he started winning trophies in weight-lifting contests, he found himself more and more at the center of attention among his friends and classmates. Before long, Arnold began to develop a correspondingly bigger sense of his own merits. Becoming a winner "supplied me with something I had been craving. I'm not sure why I had this need for special attention. Perhaps it was because I had an older brother who'd received more than his share of attention from our father."[20] It is equally likely that the accolades Arnold was already receiving served to affirm for him that his chosen life's work was the right one.

Oddly enough, it was a career path that few knew anything about. At the time, there were fewer than 50 bodybuilders in the entire country of Austria! Another likely reason for Arnold's hunger for both the attention and for the training was that they both provided immediate gratification for him. He had the kind of body that grew quickly and efficiently. And he had the kind of mentality that thrived on self-discipline, individualism, and what he called "the utter integrity of bodybuilding."[21]

One consequence of Arnold's strange obsession with such a peculiar activity was that some people saw bodybuilding as an incredibly egotistical thing to do. In his autobiography, Arnold tells about a girl with whom he developed a friendship. But when he finally asked her out on a date, she turned him down, claiming, "You're in love with yourself. You're in love with your own body."[22] To Arnold, this was a mistake that too many people made about bodybuilding and bodybuilders in general. "Nobody seemed to understand what was involved in bodybuilding. You do look at your body in a mirror, not because you are narcissistic, but because you are trying to check your progress. It has nothing to do with being in love with yourself … It just happens that the mirror, the scales, and the tape measure are the only tools a bodybuilder has for determining his progress."[23] Whereas many believed that bodybuilders must simply be feeding their over-inflated egos with oiled, mirrored reflections of their bodily beauty, for Arnold, building his body was a way to be a larger, more influential part of his world. In her book, *Bodymakers*, Leslie Heywood writes, "For Arnold, bodybuilding is about space: power, domain, prerogative, the physical space his body takes up, and the precedence granted to it in the world."[24]

But Arnold did not let such misconceptions deter him or distract him: if people did not understand his training methods and practices, that was their problem. His gym workouts had taught Arnold a "three-part formula" that would guide his career and his life: "self-confidence, a positive mental attitude, and honest hard work."[25] Ironically, despite the fact that Arnold was lifting enormous amounts of weights and training for hours and hours each day, his mother accused him of being lazy because his training regimen took precedence over ordinary household chores.

When he was barely 17 years old, Arnold not only won the Junior Mr. Austria competition, but he placed third in the adult Mr. Austria portion of the competition. Judges were impressed that such a youngster had already developed such manly musculature. But this wasn't enough for Arnold. Not nearly enough. At age 18, he still felt his body was underdeveloped. He felt constrained by what he called "the Austrian mentality in bodybuilding," which emphasized big arms and a huge chest with far too little attention paid to developing the legs and all the little muscle groups that a true bodybuilder works to define, or "cut," into his physique. By all accounts, he was already a staggeringly impressive specimen of muscular development, but by the young Schwarzenegger's much, much higher standards, he was lagging behind where he wanted to be.

In 1965, Arnold joined the Austrian army to fulfill his year of mandatory service. Rather than seeing this as an interruption in his routines, Arnold saw his military service as a positive: "I liked the regimentation, the firm, rigid structure. The whole idea of uniforms and medals appealed to me." And for Arnold, the command-structure was nothing new. His father, Gustav had "always acted like a general" around the Schwarzenegger household.[26] Gustav was delighted that his son was considering a military career, and he used his influence as a former soldier to secure a special assignment for Arnold as a tank driver. Not only was this a desirable detail for Arnold, it also meant he was stationed near Graz; he would be able to continue his training.

Army life became immediately more interesting to Arnold when, just a few weeks after he was inducted, he was invited to enter the junior division of the Mr. Europe contest to be held in Stuttgart, Germany. This was a golden opportunity for the 18-year-old bodybuilder to prove himself in an arena larger than the local Austrian venues. It also presented a significant problem for Arnold. He was in the midst of basic training and was required to remain on the base for the entire six weeks of the training period. Arnold could miss the contest, or he could do what he always did—refuse to be held back from his larger goals. In dramatic fashion, he chose the latter, deciding to sneak out of camp and travel to Germany for the contest. After climbing over a wall with barely enough money for his train ticket, he made the slow journey into Stuttgart.

Arnold claims, in his autobiography, that when he initially stood before the judges, his mind went blank, but his poses were so impressive—if amateurish—that he was called out a second time for a "pose-off" with other contestants. A few minutes later, Arnold Schwarzenegger was pronounced Mr. Europe Junior. "I felt like King Kong,"[27] he recalls, before adding that he then had to face the consequences of having gone AWOL from the army. After borrowing money to buy a return ticket to his base, he was arrested as he climbed back over the wall and put in the stockade for a week. Upon his release, he half-expected his superior officers to remain angry with him, but to his surprise he learned that his trophy had brought some positive publicity to the army. Apparently, his superiors wanted to see Arnold's training continued so he did that as part of his army duties. As a result, by the time he had completed his year of service, he had put on 25 additional pounds of muscle. The year was 1966, and Arnold was just 19 years old.

THE MONSTER FROM MUNICH

It didn't take long after Arnold's Mr. Europe Junior victory for the bodybuilding world to start to take notice of this huge newcomer to the sport. One of the judges from the contest was a gym owner and magazine publisher in Munich, and he approached Arnold with an offer to work in the gym, managing the health and bodybuilding club. The man offered to pay Arnold's way to London the following year to watch the Mr. Universe competition. Arnold's reaction was typical. He told his would-be benefactor that he had no intention of being a mere spectator; he intended to compete. So Arnold moved to Munich, Germany, to work at the gym and to push his own training to the next level.

Munich was a bit intimidating to Arnold—at least at first. The streets were crowded and noisy, and Arnold knew no one. Still, he intended to stick it out and make this experience another step on his journey to fame, and to America. One of the things Arnold learned in Munich was that bodybuilding did not discriminate between heterosexual and homosexual bodybuilders. All could be found training together at the gym, and occasionally, a wealthy man might come to the gym to "pick up" one or another of the young bodybuilders.

While some of the men accepted these propositions, Arnold notes that he "was never sorry I turned down the offers I had."

Indeed, so independent was the young Schwarzenegger that he rented himself a tiny room in someone's apartment and lived as frugally as possible. He didn't dare tell his parents that he was struggling, and instead he told them he was doing fine and earning a good living. In a way, he was telling the truth—at least in the sense that he was focused, and he was around the gym all day long, so he could train as much as he liked. "At that point, my own thinking was tuned in to only one thing: becoming Mr. Universe."[28] One of the obstacles to Arnold's own training was that he had to work as a trainer to others, and almost nothing made him more impatient than working with "people who would never benefit from what I told them" and who were "doing sissy workouts, pampering themselves."[29]

To ensure that he got his own training hours in, he began to split his training schedule into morning and evening workouts. This split routine would later become a kind of trademark of Arnold's, but at first he did it simply to work around his salaried activities during the day. For 2 hours every morning and another 2 hours every night, Arnold lifted and trained and, after just 2 months of the routine, put on another 5 pounds of muscle. Arnold had discovered that by splitting his routine, he was fresher in the evening and could lift much more weight than if he trained for 4 or 5 continuous hours. This would be one of many examples of Arnold's custom-designing workout routines and practices that would yield groundbreaking results.

When Arnold arrived at the Mr. Europe contest in Germany, he was a very big young man of 19 years. Already there were rumors circulating about the "monster from Munich"[30] who had the huge arms and chest and who was not even 20 years old. According to Arnold, when he hit his first pose—a "double biceps" — "the judges almost fainted."[31] There was a sense that history was being made, and that the newcomer named Arnold Schwarzenegger was literally running away with the entire competition. He so thoroughly dominated the contest that the officials sponsored his ticket to the Mr. Universe contest to be held in London. Before that contest, however, Arnold went on to win the competition for Best Built Man of Europe. He had come a long, long way from Thal, Austria, and his next major bodybuilding stop was not just another step on the stairway to stardom; it was the Mr. Universe contest itself. As author of *Bodymaking* Heywood argued, Arnold's body was constructed ... to stand for his ability to take over the world."[32]

Knowing almost no English, and never having traveled much beyond Austria and Germany, Arnold arrived in London for the contest and was struck immediately by the size of the bodybuilders waiting around the Royal Hotel. "They were monstrous," Arnold recalls, and they were from all over the world—India, Africa, and, of course, the United States. When these guys saw Arnold enter the hotel, they crowded around him, wanting to take stock of the young man with the "best built body" in Europe. Arnold's ego swelled, and he began to entertain the idea that he was not only going to compete, but that maybe he was going to be able to win a Mr. Universe title in his first try!

A man named Chet Yorton quickly ended Arnold's fantasy. Yorton was the favorite from America and, like Arnold, was huge. But unlike Arnold, Yorton had a look that was the kind the judges considered essential: suntanned, dramatically "cut up" with every muscle and sinew standing out, and mapped thoroughly with veins. As experienced bodybuilders had learned, when the veins stood out on the body, it meant that the body-builder had reduced his body-fat to nearly zero and pumped his muscles to the maximum. Arnold might have been discouraged by Yorton's obvious superiority, but that was not Arnold's style. Instead, Arnold, the "nineteen year old pup with the Albert Speer haircut"[33] recognized at once that, as big and strong as he was already, he was once again going to have to go back to the drawing board and train even harder. He had built himself up to be gigantic, but that was just the foundation. Now he was going to have to shape himself, cut new lines into his physique, and redefine himself. And he was going to have to get a suntan!

What Arnold had learned was that bodybuilding was not only a sport, but also an art and a science that required constant experimentation and study. But he learned something else at that 1966 Mr. Universe contest; he learned that he was a lot closer to being the best than he had previously realized. Bodybuilding contests were usually held over 2 days; the first day is for pre-judging, which is when the judges have an opportunity to really study and rate each bodybuilder. By the end of the pre-judging days, the officials have selected the winners. The second day is the public event where the bodybuilders get to show off and pose for the awe-struck crowds. At that event, Arnold discovered that he'd made quite an impression on the judges and the public. He was asked to come back out for an encore after his preliminary routine, and the cheers he received got him as pumped up as his workouts did. When Chet Yorton followed Arnold's encore with his own routine, Arnold saw in Yorton a true champion. Yorton had already won Mr. California, Mr. America (twice), and had received awards and trophies even for individual parts of his body.

That Mr. Universe contest marked a critical moment for Arnold Schwarzenegger. As usual, he took from his "defeat" (he came in second) an invaluable set of lessons. For one thing, he now knew that he would have to begin sculpting his body much more strategically.

His calves and thighs needed more work, and he would have to work on his posing routines to make even more of an impression with his body. While others assured Arnold that he would most likely win the next year's Mr. Universe contest, Arnold took nothing for granted. He knew he would have to work to master each and every element of bodybuilding if he wanted to be the best in the world. The road would be a difficult and physically painful one, but Arnold was not the least bit concerned that he would not be able to do the work. "What I had more than anyone else was drive. I was hungrier than anybody."[34]

PAIN ... AND GAIN

It is important to pause a moment here and remember that by this point, not quite 20 years old, Arnold had just earned second place at his very first international Mr. Universe contest. He accomplished this through hard training, self-designed workouts, and sheer force of will. But there was at least one other factor in Arnold's life that helped him to make such incredible progress: He knew how to capitalize on virtually every opportunity that came along. When he returned to Munich to pick up his twice-a-day training schedule, the man whose gym Arnold had been managing decided to sell the business. As Arnold had become not only his trusted manager, but also something of a local celebrity, he was given first shot at buying the gym. Of course, Arnold had very little money, but he had plenty of energy and diligence. He took on additional work, began selling nutritional supplements, giving private instruction, personal training, and more. At last, he'd raised and borrowed enough money to buy the gym. Now the challenge would be to keep it open and running.

From his high school days, Arnold had kept up an avid interest in business, and now he had his own business to grow. With his previous knowledge and an uncanny marketing sense, he made the most of his excellent showing in the Mr. Universe contest as a way to draw in new clients to the gym. In a short time, he tripled the membership. He competed in a minor contest in Essen, Germany, and won almost without effort. Once again, the local media lavished attention on Arnold, and gym membership grew even more. Then, he received a letter from London that would provide yet another vitally important component in Arnold's quest for greatness. The letter was an invitation, one of many he would receive that year, from one of the Mr. Universe judges, Wag Bennett, asking Arnold to pose in a bodybuilding exhibition. This was a new thing for Arnold. Up until then, bodybuilding was a competitive sport, not a pageant (though there was certainly plenty of exhibitionism required in a bodybuilding contest). Nevertheless, Arnold was sufficiently intrigued by this potential opportunity to broaden his bodybuilding network that he accepted the invitation.

Although Arnold was continually learning from each encounter with the bodybuilding world, and while he was always willing to find lessons in every experience of adversity, he did have an obstinate side to him. It was that obstinacy that nearly pre-empted a wonderful opportunity offered by Wag on Arnold's arrival in London. Bennett and his wife set Arnold up to stay with them in their home; Bennett wanted to help Arnold with his posing routines, and to help propel him toward greater achievement in bodybuilding. His idea was for Arnold to start posing to music, an idea that Arnold initially resisted with a stubbornness that nearly cost him. But Wag was persistent and eventually wore Arnold down. He explained that music would help Arnold smooth out his poses and transitions between poses, and that music would enhance the sense of showmanship so necessary in bodybuilding competitions. The music Wag chose for Arnold was the soundtrack from the 1960 movie *Exodus*, which depicted the founding of Israel.

Arnold dove into this new kind of training with tremendous energy. At his first London exhibition, he was amazed at the results of this intensive rehearsal. The audience loved him, and he knew he had found something that he could use. "Now bodybuilding did become show business for me. I bought *Exodus* and took it everywhere I went. I acted like a real professional, bringing my own music, telling the stage manager what lights to use and when to open and close the curtains. That's my style. As soon as I grasp something, I take control."[35] He also was taking the bodybuilding world by storm, signing autographs and having new nicknames bestowed on him, names like "the Austrian Oak," and "the Giant of Austria." Arnold reports in his autobiography that newspaper articles were saying things like, "if Hercules were to be born today his name would be Arnold Schwarzenegger."[36] That would prove to be a prescient remark, for just a few years later, Arnold would be cast in his first film—as Hercules.

At the heart of all of this activity was one constant: Arnold continued to train, harder and harder, lifting heavier and heavier weights, pushing himself beyond his previous physical limits. Every workout involved pain. Every morning he would train through the soreness from the workout the evening before. Every exercise he did, he imagined he was adding to the layers of strength and fitness he would need to be the world's best. Just as his boyhood idol, Reg Park, had done, Arnold made power-lifting an integral part of his training and his bodybuilding philosophy.

Muscles grow as they recover from specific stresses placed on them. When, for example, you lift weights, the muscles develop micro-tears in the muscle fibers. During periods of rest and recovery, as the muscles heal themselves, they grow extra muscle cells to help prevent further "damage." Bodybuilders who lift enormous amounts of weight for many, many repetitions are constantly "tearing up" their muscles. During their recovery periods, bodybuilders then grow much more muscle fiber, creating much larger muscles over time. It's similar to what happens when you cut yourself. As the skin and tissue heal, the cut closes. But the healing process tends to overcompensate, and scar tissue develops. If you were regularly to go barefoot outdoors, your feet would become raw and then heal themselves by developing a little extra in the form of calluses. Training your muscles causes microscopic trauma to those muscles, and the body repairs this trauma by healing the muscle cells and then increasing the overall size and density of the muscle.

Power lifting means pain. The pain of tiny muscle fibers breaking and rebuilding themselves, the pain of large muscles lurching up and out as they strained to hoist and hold outrageously heavy steel plates, the agony of muscles fighting failure as they filled with lactic acid, the burning pain of exhausted muscles being pushed for one more set, one more repetition. This was Arnold's daily experience, and it was this willingness to drive his way into and through pain that propelled him to place so highly at the Mr. Universe contest. As 1966 came to an end, Arnold had proven to himself that he was a bona fide member of the international bodybuilding elite. But there was much more work to be done.

Early in 1967, Arnold wrote to Reg Park, and to his surprise, Park answered. Park invited Arnold to meet him in London to do an exhibition together. The two met and each was quite impressed with the other. Arnold knew that his hero's physique had elements that were essential for championship bodybuilding, the muscle groups that a bodybuilder must have if he is to emerge as better than the rest. Arnold increased the intensity of his training, and learned all he could from Reg. Meeting Reg Park had at least one other profound effect on Arnold: he made Arnold want to be "a better person" —one who was less aggressive and more secure in knowing he was the best, someone who did not have to prove his worth every time he competed. He no longer had to act like a tough guy because he had already proven to himself and to others that he was tough, hard working, and totally devoted to his training. He was, in a way, a new man.

MR. UNIVERSE ... AND BEYOND!

Just before he entered his second Mr. Universe (NABBA Amateur) contest in 1967, Arnold took stock of himself and of the key factors that had brought him to the brink of international fame. He came up with a list of five factors. First, he had the right kind of body for the type of training he was doing. "My bone structure was perfect—long legs, long arms, long torso. Plus everything was in proportion. It fell together and flowed."

Second, he had always been able to make use of every aspect of his upbringing, good and bad. Things he didn't get as a child just made him "hungry" for them as an adult. Third, he had begun his bodybuilding training in a part of the world where "there was nothing else going on" to distract him. Fourth, Arnold maintained a positive attitude at all times and trained every week of every year. Fifth, "I was honest with myself about what my body looked like and where I'd have to improve."[37]

It was time to bring everything together—the posing, the body sculpting, the pump-up, the muscle mass, and something Arnold noticed missing from many other bodybuilding presentations and routines: smoothness of movement. Arnold was determined not only to be a winner, but to be perfect. This time around at the contest, Arnold would also be adding an element he'd left out of the last one: the psych-out. The man to beat that year was the latest Mr. America, Dan Tinnerino. Many considered Tinnerino the heir apparent to Chet Yorton. Arnold has said that fellow bodybuilder Ricky Wayne told him that Tinnerino looked so good, Arnold didn't have a chance to beat him. But Wayne, in his own book wrote that Arnold's NABBA win in London in 1967, "had to be the most predictable in the history of NABBA."[38]

The morning of pre-judging, Arnold had a chance to meet and talk with Tinnerino. According to Arnold's autobiography, when Tinnerino asked Arnold how he was, Arnold replied, "Fantastic!" and then added, "It's the kind of day when you know you're going to win." Needless to say, Arnold was in the right frame of mind to win, and win he did. "I wiped everybody, including Tinnerino, off the stage. I got the best reaction—it was the first time I remember people really screaming, 'Arnold! Arnold! '"[39] Afterward, people made comments that pleased Arnold. They called him a monster and an animal, flattering terms for a bodybuilder. Arnold had beaten 90 of the world's best. He was 20 years old.

So what could be beyond "Mr. Universe?" The answer: Mr. Universe. Shortly before the NABBA Mr. Universe contest, another, new Mr. Universe contest was created. This one was run by the IFBB, and the winner of that contest had been the Cuban bodybuilder, Sergio Oliva. Now there were three Mr. Universes: Arnold had won the NABBA Amateur competition; Oliva was the IFBB Mr. Universe, and Bill Pearl was the NABBA Professional Mr. Universe. To make matters still more competitive, Ricky Wayne was the reigning Mr. World, and Sergio Oliva had also won the Mr. Olympia competition.

Arnold now had a new set of challenges. It was one thing to be the best amateur bodybuilder in the world. Now he had to be the "ultimate winner" of all competitions. To accomplish this, Arnold would have to return to the gym and work harder than ever before. He returned to Germany, entering an exhibition in Stuttgart, which gave his father an opportunity to watch his son strike classic Olympian poses. When the crowd went wild, Gustav understood, perhaps for the first time, just how much his son had already achieved in this strange world of bodybuilding.

After his Mr. Universe win, Reg Park invited Arnold to stay with him and his wife in Johannesburg, South Africa, and to do an exhibition. While staying with Park, Arnold got a chance to see just how hard his mentor trained and how Park had been able to add the refinements to his muscles that had made him such a champion. On his return to Munich, Arnold knew he would have to find a way to train that would catapult him above and beyond what anyone else in bodybuilding was doing.

SHOCK AND AWE ... AND MORE PAIN

Now everyone wanted to train with Arnold Schwarzenegger, and his gym memberships were growing geometrically. With a crew of fellow workout junkies around him, Arnold began a training course that dwarfed any previous experience with pain. Indeed, the new workouts would entail torturous routines that required pushing beyond the physical agony. Arnold's new idea for training was, he realized, a system of "shocking the muscles." Instead of a regular routine of, say, 10 sets of military presses, Arnold would do 50 sets. If the usual workout entailed 20 sets of squats with weights, the shock-workout might include 50 or 60 sets. Some of these workouts left Arnold and his training partners barely able to walk, but his legs were growing.

These new workouts also involved a new decadence that Arnold writes briefly about in his autobiography. He and fellow bodybuilders would take their weights and barbells to the woods, along with beer and food and, of course, women. They'd train for hours, go for a naked swim, eat food and drink wine and beer, and then train some more. As he readily admits, the training at that point became "pure insanity"; the guys would be dropping weights and falling down. But no matter how crazy things got, at the core of it all was Arnold's fierce determination to out-do everyone in the bodybuilding world, no matter how much pain was required to get there. And these new shock workouts were a new form of pain, a new level of excruciating training. "We were breaking through the pain barrier and shocking the muscle."[40]

Arnold was developing a truly awesome body using methods entirely of his own design. Others could do the workouts with him—or try to—but it was always Arnold who pushed harder, farther, lifted more weight, did more sets, withstood more pain. He seemed indestructible, a "walking billboard of invulnerability."[41] That year, 1967, Arnold entered the annual stone lifting contest in Munich, where contestants would grab the steel handle and lift a stone block weighing more than 500 pounds as high as they could. Arnold shattered the existing record and was dubbed the strongest man in Germany. This was important to Arnold mainly because he had always insisted that bodybuilders must be more than cosmetic musclemen; they must be genuinely strong men as well.

Few men in modern history have been as driven as Arnold Schwarzenegger was at that time. He still had his sights set on coming to America and becoming the world's most dominant and recognized body-builder. As important and intensive as his physical training was, he knew that what was going to get him to the topmost level of bodybuilding and to all his other goals as well was the power of his mind. He knew he would win Mr. Universe in London again in 1968 because he was supremely confident of both is physical and mental preparation. This time, however, his victory threw open a new door of opportunity for him, the chance he'd been waiting for. Joe Weider, bodybuilding magazine publisher (of *Muscle Builder* and *Mr. America*, at that time) and bodybuilding promoter invited Arnold to compete in his IFBB Mr. Universe contest to be held in Miami, Florida. Arnold would now have sponsorship, through Weider, to train in the United States and compete for one more coveted prize. It was an opportunity that would awe anyone, anyone except Arnold. For Arnold, it was the expected outcome of a decade of pain, soreness, discipline, cleverness, determination, and hunger. He was going to America where he planned to shock the world.

UNSTOPPABLE

Arnold was entering a phase of his life where he would become unstoppable. But first, he had to experience something relatively foreign to him: He was stopped. Cold. Arnold had probably out-trained everybody in the IFBB contest, but he still knew relatively little about the kinds of nutrition and drugs being used in the highest echelons of bodybuilding. According to Rick Wayne, when Mr. Olympia Larry Scott retired in 1966, his response to a reporter's question, "Have you ever taken steroids?" was, without hesitation, "Sure … doesn't everyone? They've become a regular part of bodybuilding in the states."[42]

Arnold knew that in America he would learn these things, just as he had learned, as a teenager training in Graz at Marnul's gym, that steroids were just part of what bodybuilders were expected to use for their craft. He also knew that he was very good already and that the Florida contest would be a great way to prove this to Americans. Fellow bodybuilder Rick Wayne described his sighting of Arnold at the contest: "He seemed damned sure of himself, full of Aryan contempt. You could tell by his stage manner, his pigeon-toed strut, the way he carried his enormous chest, that privately he held himself above ... the other Mr. Universe contenders."[43] As expected, the crowds loved the 22-year-old and found his finely sculpted body very impressive. But before long, Arnold became aware that the contest was much closer than he'd anticipated. A bodybuilder by the name of Frank Zane was wowing the judges with his perfectly chiseled body, and although Zane was competing as a medium-height bodybuilder, he took first place and was crowned Mr. Universe. Bigger was not better that day, or as Rick Wayne put, "Mass does not necessarily spell class,"[44] and second-place winner Arnold was so devastated, he felt he had let everyone down. He had been stopped. But only for the briefest of moments.

What followed that "loss" in Miami was a run of bodybuilding triumphs that would truly stagger the bodybuilding world. Joe Weider agreed to support Arnold for another year in the United States where Arnold intended to "beat everybody in America."[45] Along the way, Arnold was going to learn everything he could about business—both bodybuilding and business in general. Weider would pay Arnold a salary in exchange for Arnold's training tips and the use of his image for photographs in Weider's magazines. Not satisfied to rely on someone else for income, Arnold started up his own mail order business selling, among other things, bodybuilding nutritional supplements. And, of course, he trained. He would not be stopped again.

By the time the 1969 Mr. Universe contest came up in New York City that fall, Arnold was "cut and chiseled and tanned" and ready to take on anyone and everyone. But not *everyone* was there. Sergio Oliva was entered in the Mr. Olympia contest being held the same night as Mr. Universe. (Oliva had already won the Mr. Olympia twice in a row.) This angered Arnold because he'd been counting on beating the entire field of contestants, especially the one they called, "the Myth."[46] Now it was looking like Oliva had eluded Schwarzenegger. But Arnold would not be stopped or avoided. He managed to get himself entered into the Mr. Olympia contest to be held after the Mr. Universe! Arnold easily won the IFBB Mr. Universe competition, garnering unanimous votes from all the judges. Then it was time to rush off to the Mr. Olympia.

In the dressing room, he got his first up-close look at Sergio Oliva and knew, right then and there, that Oliva was—at least for now—the better man. Oliva was absolutely huge, ripped, and confident. It bothered Arnold less to have to take second place in that contest, especially since the decision had been extremely close.

Arnold now had one more reason to continue training in America, and he set his mind to coming back a year later to defeat Oliva. In the meantime, he zipped over to London to enter NABBA's Mr. Universe contest and beat everyone, winning his second Mr. Universe title in one year, and his fourth overall. Arnold was on the hunt. He got Joe Weider to sponsor him for another year in the States and to bring over his good friend, Franco Columbu, to be his training partner. Arnold had always found that training with Franco meant being able to push himself beyond all previous limits and to add yet another dimension to his training, Arnold began working with a ballet instructor to perfect his posing movements. The only thing that could possibly get in Arnold's way now was Arnold himself.

In 1970, Arnold returned to London for the Mr. Universe contest and was shocked to discover that he would be competing against none other than his hero, Reg Park! In his autobiography, Arnold wrote that he had two choices: he could beat Reg and, possibly, humiliate his idol, or he could leave London and not compete. Arnold was on the verge of stopping himself on his journey to be the world's most dominant and feared bodybuilder. But there was to be no more stopping Arnold Schwarzenegger, and he made the decision to compete—and to win. Reg Park placed second. Arnold was on a roll.

The very next day, Arnold flew to Columbus, Ohio, to compete in the Mr. World contest, where, much to Arnold's surprise, he found Sergio Oliva already entered in the competition. Oliva looked good, but Arnold looked better. He was more ripped, more cut, more pumped. Oliva was announced as the second place winner, and Arnold was declared the winner. At that moment, Arnold was the conqueror of all the world's greatest bodybuilders. Two weeks later, at the Mr. Olympia, odds-makers called it even between Schwarzenegger and Oliva. But Arnold was unstoppable, and he was crowned Mr. Olympia, as well. In what is considered "the Super Bowl of bodybuilding," Arnold reigned supreme. "I was King Kong."[47]

Some time later, in an interview for a magazine, Arnold was asked, "This business of feeling like King Kong—is it your act to psych everyone out so they know you're King Kong?" Arnold replied that he simply uses his powerful presence to make others "… feel great. I tell a guy that he's never looked better, that he looks brilliant, fantastic … I'm positive that you'll place … You can easily beat this guy and that guy. I'm certain you'll go all the way—to second place."[48]

Arnold went on to win a total of five different Mr. Universe titles, Mr. World, IFBB Mr. International, and six Mr. Olympias in a row from 1970 to 1975. In 1980, Arnold came out of retirement to win his seventh Mr. Olympia in Sydney Australia, a contest that Rick Wayne called "the most controversial in the history of the Olympia."[49] Arnold had been a last minute entry, and some thought the judging was too sympathetic toward the 33-year-old former champion. There were even rumors that the contest was fixed. But as early as that 1970 Mr. World title, Arnold felt that he had already proven to the world that he was the greatest bodybuilder of all time.

ARNOLD AFTER ARNOLD

Whatever bodybuilding was before Arnold, it's safe to say that it was changed forever after Arnold. When the bodybuilding documentary, *Pumping Iron*, came out in 1977, it sparked a worldwide passion for weight training and for Arnold himself. Memberships at fitness clubs and gyms shot up. Movie producers had all but given up on making any more muscle movies, but now Arnold had single handedly resurrected the genre while also reconfiguring America's ideas about muscles, bodies, and masculinity. Now, more than ever, bodybuilding was seen as an art form, and a super-muscular body was viewed as an object of desire. Books were published on bodybuilding, weight training, and fitness, and the whole gym industry grew and grew. Big muscles were now a sign of hard work, self-discipline, self-improvement, and admirable power.

Arnold´s fame also grew. In the bodybuilding world, he was a god—*the* god. He had redefined size, training regimens, symmetry, and dedication to victory. He forever changed people's minds about the bodybuilder as brainless musclehead. He was smart, funny, charismatic, clever, and savvy in ways few celebrities were.

Unfortunately, with the renewed interest in bodybuilding came an increase in drug use as a means of more quickly developing muscle. A doctor and scientist by the name of John Ziegler, who once worked with the United States Olympic team, had developed a way of manipulating testosterone, the male hormone, and making it more effective in enhancing muscular development. He called his new product Dianabol, an early form of anabolic steroid that would come to be used and abused throughout the bodybuilding, and ultimately the entire sports, world. The excessive use of steroids among bodybuilders throughout the 1980s undermined nearly all the gains of respectability from earlier decades. Of course, many if not most of the earlier champion bodybuilders had used steroids as well, but the extent of steroid use reached unimaginable proportions in the years following Arnold's retirement.

Arnold himself has been eclipsed in size by the subsequent generations of massively developed, steroid-pumping bodybuilders of the past two and a half decades. And yet in some ways his body is bigger now than it ever has been, bigger than when he was Mr. Olympia, with "a physique that strained the imagination."[50] This may be a curious statement because anyone who looks at Arnold now can easily see that in terms of body mass, he has become quite noticeably shrunken in the last 20 years. It is what Arnold's body can do now that makes him so big. Arnold has become a dominant icon in America because *his* body is the one we think of when we want to describe something larger than life. Within his current frame are images that include the impossibly hard laborer, the immigrant-made-good, the uncannily clever financial planner, the quintessential consumer capitalist who understood how to turn his body into a powerful commodity, and the master planner whose charted course brought him to the capitol of California.

Even today, in his relatively diminished bodily form, Arnold remains the standard by which the real and metaphorical size of others is measured. As Susan Faludi has claimed in her book on American manhood, "The ordinary man is no fool: he knows he can't be Arnold Schwarzenegger."[51] But long before Arnold's body was trimmed down to a smaller, older size, he was still basking in his early victories over all of the major bodybuilders in the world. He was going to strike, again, while the iron was hot and his muscles pumped. It was time for new vistas. The man who had remade bodybuilding in his own image was about to embark on the next leg of his colossal journey to super-stardom.

NOTES

1. Hillary MacGregor, "In Japan, He's Larger Than Larger-Than-Life," *Los Angeles Times*, November 19, 2003, p. E2.

2. Jerry Schwartz, "Schwarzenegger: From Mr. Universe to Governor," *The Sacramento Bee*, October 8, 2003.

3. George Butler, *Arnold Schwarzenegger: A Portrait* (New York: Simon & Schuster, 1990), p. 13.

4. Julian Schmidt, "Arnold," *Muscle & Fitness* (August 1991): 91.

5. Bill Dobbins, "Road to Greatness" *FLEX* (July 1997): 84.

6. Butler, *Arnold Schwarzenegger*, p. 16.

7. See http://www.schwarzenegger.com/en/news/askarnold/news_askarnold_eng_legacy_441.asp?sec=news&subsec=askarnold.

8. See http://www.nicolebass.com/free/stories/biography.htm.

9. Leslie Heywood, *Bodymakers: A Cultural Anatomy of Women's Body Building* (Rutgers, NJ: Rutgers University Press, 1998), p. 66.

10. Michael S. Kimmel, "Consuming Manhood: The Feminization of American Culture and the Re-creation of the Male Body, 1823–1920," in *The Male Body: Features, Destinies, Exposures*, Ed. Laurence Goldstein. (Ann Arbor: University of Michigan Press, 1994), p. 22.

11. David L. Chapman, "Sandow: the Man Who Made the World Mad for Muscles," 2001. Accessed July 26, 2006, http://www.sandowmuseum.com/sandowtwo.html.

12. Ibid., p. 13.

13. Ibid., p. 16.

14. Ibid., p. 17.

15. Ibid., p. 19.

16. Ibid., p. 19.

17. Nigel Andrews, *True Myths: The Life and Times of Arnold Schwarzenegger* (Seacaucus, NJ: Carol Publishing, 1995), p. 18.

18. Arnold Schwarzenegger and Douglas Kent Hall, *Arnold: The Education of a Bodybuilder* (New York: Simon & Schuster, 1977), p. 34.

19. Ibid., p. 23.

20. Ibid., p. 24.

21. Ibid., p. 26.

22. Ibid., p. 27.

23. Ibid., p. 27.

24. Heywood, *Bodymakers*, p. 46.

25. Schwarzenegger and Kent Hall, *Arnold*, p. 30.

26. Ibid., p. 35.

27. Ibid., p. 37.

28. Ibid., p. 43.

29. Ibid., p. 44.

30 Ibid., p.45.

31. Ibid., p. 45.

32. Heywood, *Bodymakers*, p. 48.

33. Rick Wayne, *Muscle Wars: The Behind the Scenes Story of Competitive Bodybuilding* (New York: St. Martin's Press, 1985), p. 59.

34. Schwarzenegger and Kent Hall, *Arnold*, p.53.

35. Ibid., pp. 58–59.

36. Ibid.

37. Ibid., pp. 67–68.

38. Wayne, *Muscle Wars*, p. 98.

39. Schwarzenegger and Kent Hall, *Arnold*, p. 75.

40. Ibid., p. 85.

41. Heywood, *Bodymakers*, p. 48.

42. Wayne, *Muscle Wars*, p. 88.

43. Ibid., p.104.

44. Ibid.

45. Schwarzenegger and Kent Hall, *Arnold*, p. 94.

46. See http://www.sergiooliva.com.

47. Schwarzenegger and Kent Hall, *Arnold*, p. 106.

48. Colette Bancroft, "Arnold the Contender: King Kong or Fay Wray?," *St. Petersburg Times Online*, September 5, 2003: http://www.sptimes.com/2003/09/05/news_pf/Floridian/Arnold_the_contender_.shtml.

49. Wayne, *Muscle Wars*, p. 158.

50. Arnold Schwarzenegger. Interview with Bill Hemmer. *People in the News*. CNN. July 12, 2003. Accessed July 26, 2006, http://transcripts.cnn.com/TRANSCRIPTS/0307/12/pitn.00.html.

51. Susan Faludi, *Stiffed: The Betrayal of the American Man* (New York: William Morrow and Company, 1999,) p. 35.

Chapter 4

FROM HERCULES TO HOLLYWOOD

The urge to be associated with the gods has been an integral part of Western civilization for centuries. In ancient Greece (about 1000 B.C. to about 100 B.C.), the gods were thought to look like humans, but they had powers much like our superheroes of today. There were hundreds of gods but only 12 primary ones, the Olympians, who were the most powerful and most admired. They lived atop Mt. Olympus, a real mountain in Greece and the country's highest point. These gods had unique powers and abilities but also had human characteristics. They could control the lives of mere mortals, as well as the elements and the fates, sometimes playfully and sometimes with a vengeance. Zeus, Hera, Poseidon, Hermes, and Athena were all Olympians, and the Olympic Games were originally held to honor them.

There was also a belief in demigods in the time of the ancient Greeks. They were the offspring of a god and a human. Heracles was the name of one of the demigods, and he became one of the most admired heroic figures of that time. He is one of the ancient Greek figures to have survived through the centuries in heroic stories and myths. Today, we know him as Hercules, and he has remained a popular hero in everything from Disney cartoons to low-budget movie epics.

The mythological stories told about the gods were first memorized and told orally. They also appeared in images, painting, mosaics, statues, and pottery. The stories were then written down. We can still read these stories and see this artwork today. But with the invention of the motion picture around 1900, the stories of the gods became animated, and the movies have provided us with a century of superheroic figures based on the same stories that the ancient Greeks believed in.

In the 1950s and 1960s, mythological characters like Hercules and Samson were common in low-budget movies that were sometime known as sword-and-sandal epics. Popular throughout the world, many of these were made in Italy, and some were dubbed in English so that even the actors who spoke English had different voices.

The Hercules movies called for men of epic proportions, men with bodies that were not normally associated with mere mortals. These sword-and-sandal epics featured some of the best bodybuilders of the era like Reg Park and Steve Reeves, and they are said to have inspired Arnold Schwarzenegger, Lou Ferrigno, and Sylvester Stallone to pursue both bodybuilding and movie careers.

While it was the handsome Steve Reeves who starred in *Hercules* in 1958 and *Hercules Unchained* in 1959 that made muscled guys in ancient skimpy clothes a box office hit, it was Reg Park who made the biggest impression on Arnold. As a young man, Arnold admired Park who eventually starred in four Hercules and one Samson film from 1961 to 1965. In his autobiography, Arnold says he was obsessed with Park, putting his pictures all over his bedroom and following his training program and diet. When Arnold first walked into a gym, he was awed by the bodybuilders, describing them as "powerful looking, Herculean."[1]

Arnold worked hard to be like Reg Park; Park's use of his muscular body to conquer the world through the movies appealed to Arnold. When Arnold explained to his father why he was building a muscular body, he said that after he became the "best-built man in the world," he wanted to be in the movies, in America, just like Reg Park.

So when Arnold was later encouraged by both Reg Park and his business associate Joe Weider to do a movie called, *Hercules in New York,* it was not an unusual course for the young bodybuilder to take. Arnold's dream to enter the larger world of heroic movie stardom and mythological status were about to come true.

ARNOLD STRONG

Hercules in New York became Arnold's first starring role and another means of getting his well-built body into the public's view. But rather than being a faithful representation of some ancient myth like Reg Park's movies, *Hercules in New York* placed the demigod into Manhattan and used a fish-out-of-water motif to place Arnold in odd and silly situations that usually required him to take his shirt off, to fight, or both. Hercules had to overcome a bear in Central Park, longshoremen, taxi drivers, and college boys as he learned about the mortal world.

Arnold's voiced was dubbed because he could not speak English clearly. A re-release of this cult favorite on DVD in the 1990s included the original soundtrack with Arnold's heavily accented voice. Arnold's acting was horrible. He starred (under the corny stage name "Arnold Strong") opposite the famous comic figures and voice of many cartoon characters, Arnold Stang. Stang's scrawny physique and whiny character was the perfect foil, making Arnold look bigger, more masculine, and more powerful. By 2005, thousands of users of the Web site Internet Movie Database (IMDb.com) had voted *Hercules in New York* as #59 on the list of the 100 worst movies ever made.

To say the least, *Hercules in New York* was not a big hit. That year, moviegoers instead went to see romantic dramas like *Love Story* and *Airport*, the cinema verité of John Cassavetes in *Husbands*, and sophisticated comedies like *M*A*S*H*. Sword-and-sandal epics were passé. But Arnold had a taste of the dream he had seen his idols achieve: movie stardom after his bodybuilding career ended.

The next year, 1970, several of the major bodybuilding competitions were held close together. Arnold had to compete in the Mr. Universe contest one week before the Mr. Olympia contest. To his surprise, his major competitor there was his old idol, Reg Park, who came out of retirement for one last contest. Arnold, like in great mythology, defeated his idol and by winning opened the way to Mr. Olympia. Arnold achieved the ultimate honor in bodybuilding the same year he was the cinematic Hercules, earning the right in two different arenas to be seen among the pantheon of bodybuilding gods. That same year he also was Mr. Universe and Mr. World, defeating every major bodybuilder in the world and dominating a sport he was helping to redefine and shape in his own image.

Arnold's win that year, and the next four more times in a row, made him the definitive spokesman for Joe Weider's products, competitions, and training programs. Weider, who promoted bodybuilding through a series of popular magazines, featured Arnold regularly on the magazine covers and inside in lengthy stories. Both Weider and Schwarzenegger reaped large financial rewards from the collaboration.

For some people, this string of Mr. Olympia wins confirmed Arnold's place as the best bodybuilder ever. Others were not so sure as they questioned Arnold's techniques of intimidating his opponents even as he hid the flaws of his own body. But this confident strategy is what took him to the next stage of his life.

In 1974, Arnold's friends, photographer George Butler, and writer Charles Gaines, published the book *Pumping Iron*, which featured Arnold in photographs and interviews as the perfect specimen of masculine body-building. The best-selling book introduced both bodybuilding and Arnold to a whole new audience, one that was not necessarily made up of body-builders or fitness buffs. Instead, ordinary people were discovering that Arnold's story was both fascinating and inspiring regardless of the reader's personal circumstances. But was Arnold ready to move on? After the 1974 Mr. Olympia contest, there were rumors that Arnold was ready to retire. By then he had a very small role in one more film, Robert Altman's 1973 *The Long Goodbye*, but a Hollywood career did not yet seem inevitable.

STRONGMAN ARNOLD

The 1975 Mr. Olympia contest was to be held in South Africa where the now retired Reg Park lived. Butler and Gaines made a proposal to Arnold: If he competed in the 1975 Mr. Olympia contest, they would make him the focus of a "docudrama" about the process of preparing for the ultimate bodybuilding competition. If he didn't compete, they would make the movie without him, and his Hollywood ambitions would not be any closer to being fulfilled. Directed by George Butler and Robert Fiore, the movie *Pumping Iron* got good reviews both at its original release and years later when it appeared on video and DVD.

Pumping Iron was partly staged and partly a recording of actual events, but it was overall a fascinating look at an American subculture. The first part of the movie looks at the amateur Mr. Universe contest, for which Arnold was no longer eligible. The rest of the story focused on Arnold and his competition with the large, shy rival who would go on to become TV's *The Incredible Hulk*, Lou Ferrigno. Ferrigno and Schwarzenegger, along with long-time Schwarzenegger friend Franco Columbu, were the three main competitors in that year's Mr. Olympia contest.

Ferrigno was taller and bigger than Arnold, but he lacked the one qual-ity that had made Arnold so successful in bodybuilding: confidence. The movie shows Arnold undermining Ferrigno's confidence at every turn, suggesting that what wins in the competition is not the best body, but the most ruthless and single-minded competitor. Throughout *Pumping Iron*, Arnold is seen as an aggressive and somewhat devious competitor, who used several tricks to psyche out his opponents. The movie also shows that Arnold had a history of doing this, and that in many ways this is what people found compelling about him.

The movie also focused on Arnold's masculinity, showing him being the center of attention of women at the beach, in a photo studio, and at the gym. This effort to take bodybuilding out of a gay subculture and bring it into the mainstream is considered to be one of *Pumping Iron's* greatest successes and is thought by many historians of American society to be a major turning point in the development of America's fitness culture. It was also, for many people, their first introduction to the amazing character and presence of Arnold Schwarzenegger.

Charles Gaines, the writer of *Pumping Iron,* had also written the novel *Stay Hungry* about a bodybuilder before he had even met Arnold. *Stay Hungry* was going to be made into a movie, and Arnold was up for the part of Joe Santo, an ambitious bodybuilder recruited to help keep open a gym threatened by big developers. The movie starred two soon-to-be-very-famous actors, Sally Fields and Jeff Bridges, and was directed by Bob Rafelson, who was best known for his film *Five Easy Pieces* in 1970. He also directed several episodes of the television series, *The Monkees,* in the 1960s. Rafelson had a filmmaking style that perhaps epitomized the 1960s and 1970s: loose, episodic, and a bit eccentric. In his review of the movie when it came out, film critic Roger Ebert wrote that "when the movie's over, we're still not sure why it was made."[2] Nevertheless, his review was basically positive, and he saw Arnold as an interesting newcomer.

In 1976, while *Pumping Iron* was being readied for release, *Stay Hungry,* Arnold's third Hollywood film, was released to theatres. This movie, like his other two already out, was a disaster. Yet inexplicably, Arnold was awarded a Golden Globe Award for the "Best Acting Debut in a Motion Picture" by a male, even though this was not Arnold's debut and hardly a winning performance. The Golden Globes are given out by the Hollywood Foreign Press Association, a small group of mostly aged retirees working as part-time foreign journalists, who seem to wield an inordinate amount of power in Hollywood. Sylvester Stallone won that same night for *Rocky* as best picture.

Arnold was now poised to take Hollywood but still the right role had not come along. *Pumping Iron* was released in January, 1977, but after that there was nothing that seemed to fit the heavily accented voice, pumped up body, and somewhat graceless persona. With the sword-and-sandal epics gone, it seemed that Hollywood did not have a place for Arnold in an era that was focused on quality movies like *The Godfather* (1972 and 1974), *Chinatown* (1974), and *One Flew over the Cuckoo's Nest* (1975) and introduced the idea of the summer blockbuster with movies like *Jaws* (1975) and *Star Wars* (1977).

It is all the more remarkable, then, that Arnold was able to turn what appeared to be his insurmountable handicaps into the assets that would transform him from the biggest bodybuilder into, for many years, the biggest movie star in the world.

NOTES

1. Arnold Schwarzenegger and Douglas Kent Hall, *Arnold: the Education of a Bodybuilder* (New York: Simon & Schuster, 1977), back cover.

2. See Roger Ebert, "Reviews," *Sun Times*, January 1, 1976: http://rogerebert.sun-times.com/apps/pbcs.dll/article?AID=/19760101/REVIEWS/601010311/1023.

Chapter 5

MOVIE STAR ARNOLD

Movie stars, especially the important ones who occupy the "A list," the ones who are most popular and most bankable, often seem to have attained the American Dream of wealth, happiness, romance, and lots and lots of attention. Arnold Schwarzenegger stands out as a sure winner both in the dream contest and at the box office.

From his first role as Hercules to his last Terminator movie, Arnold has become a screen image that has left a variety of impressions on both critics and audiences. These films can also be seen as one component of a career that was carefully planned and executed and whose end result was the achievement of the American Dream. Arnold claimed in an interview in a UCLA student newspaper in 1982 that he could be picky about his film roles because he certainly didn't need the money like other actors did. He said, "I could wait and get projects that could help me one way or another with my career. Even when I did *The Villain*—I read the script, and I knew it was not an interesting script—I thought I would love to work with Ann-Margaret and Kirk Douglas, I could learn from them. This is the way I chose my roles: I always had to find something in the package that interested me or could move me up slowly."[1]

Here, then, in the order in which they were released, are the films Arnold Schwarzenegger had a role in and which had widespread, usually international, distribution. It is interesting to see the development in the types of roles he was offered, the number of films he released each year as he entered the prime of his career, and the rise of his box office receipts, which resulted in his becoming one of the most highly paid actors in history.[2]

Title: *Hercules in New York* (alternate titles *Hercules Goes Bananas*)
Release Date: February 25, 1970
Role: Hercules, a demi-god
Taglines:

- It's Tremendous!! It's Stupendous!! It's Fun!!
- The Legendary Hero …
- The movie with MUSCLE

Story:

In his first movie, two years after he came to California, Arnold stars (using the stage name Arnold Strong) as Hercules in a cheap and silly movie about the Greek demi-god, a character that has been played by many bodybuilders in the movies. Hercules is bored with life on Mount Olympus, but when he asks his father Zeus for permission to leave, Zeus denies his request. However, Hercules accidentally gets sent to New York by one of Zeus' thunderbolts, and there he has a series of adventures and troubles.

Hercules meets up with a scrawny, whiny New York pretzel vendor named Pritzie, played by the well-known comedian Arnold Stang, who couldn't be more different from Arnold in appearance, statures, and body proportions. Hercules gets into fights with everyone. He rides a chariot around the city and takes his shirt off every chance he gets. There isn't much of a plot, and the acting is so stilted that it is almost painful waiting for the story to progress.

Often voted one of the worst films of all time, it nevertheless opened doors in Hollywood for the future governor of California. Some fans find it incredibly funny because it is so bad; others just groan at the cheesy effects and terrible acting. As one fan explained, "If stupid things make you laugh, then this movie is a must," but another insisted, "I recommend *Hercules in New York* to anyone who likes to go to the dentist or enjoys a hard punch in the nose. This is an hour and a half of pure agony."[3]

Title: *The Long Goodbye*
Role: A member of a gang of thugs
Release Date: March 7, 1973
Taglines:

- Nothing says goodbye like a bullet.

Story:

Arnold really only had a small role, and no dialogue, in this movie by the noted director Robert Altman. Elliot Gould plays the famous detective Phillip Marlowe, who is looking for a missing person. Arnold plays one of the thugs, who beat up Marlowe because Arnold's mobster boss says Marlowe's friend owes him money.

The clip of the film on Arnold's own Web site shows a scene in which the mobster forces everyone to take off their clothes, so Marlowe can "tell me the truth about my money." The connection between this group of men undressing and the location of the money is unclear, but the scene shows a buff Arnold trying to help Marlowe remove his jacket. The clip ends with Arnold beginning to remove his jeans. Arnold was hardly a blip on the screen in this movie, and he had very little to do with the critical reception of this film or its box office.

Title: *Stay Hungry*
Role: Joe Santo, an Austrian bodybuilder
Release Date: April 23, 1976
Taglines:

 • If you've got an appetite for life: Stay Hungry

Story:

Arnold received a Golden Globe award as best newcomer of 1977 for his part in this story about Austrian bodybuilder Joe Santo, who is preparing for the Mr. Universe contest in the Olympic gym. The gym property is being sought by a developer, who sends in a rich guy named Craig Blake, played by Jeff Bridges, to secretly obtain it.

The concept of staying hungry is one that Arnold has said repeatedly is the leading philosophy of his life. In an interview with Studs Terkel for his book on American Dreams, Arnold explained, "If you have a dream and it becomes a reality, don't stay satisfied with it too long. Make up a new dream and hunt after that one and turn it into reality. When you have that dream achieved, make up a new dream."[4] Whether Arnold got the concept from this movie or the movie was demonstrating his philosophy is hard to say.

Title: *Scavenger Hunt*
Role: Lars, the gym instructor
Release Date: December 21, 1979

Taglines:

- It's a mixed-mad, merrycap mad-up mod of maniacs in a very money, merry funny movie.

Story:
Arnold is one of dozens of characters in this comedy about a man who leaves his inheritance to the relatives who can find some objects in his scavenger hunt.

Title: *The Villain*
Role: Handsome Stranger, a virtuous cowboy
Release Date: July 20, 1979

Story:
The chance to see Arnold in a skin-tight blue cowboy suit (costumes designed by Bob Mackie who did Cher's television costumes) may be the only appeal of this western/comedy. "I'm Handsome Stranger," Arnold's character says to Charming Jones (Ann-Margaret), and she replies in awe, "Yes, you are." His job is to bring to justice the bank robber Cactus Jack (Kirk Douglas) and to deliver Charming to her father, Parody. The movie was directed by former stuntman Hal Needham, and all accounts claim it was an effort to make a Roadrunner-type cartoon using live people. One viewer's verdict of the film was, "*The Villain* is first-class proof that some ideas deserve a merciless death before someone gets a chance to throw money at it and make a wider audience share the pain."[5]

Title: *Conan the Barbarian*
Release Date: May 14, 1982
Role: Conan, a Cimmerian barbarian from the north during the "Hyborian" age
Budget: $19 million
Taglines:

- He conquered an empire with his sword. She conquered HIM with her bare hands.
- Thief Warrior Gladiator King

Gross Domestic Box Office: $38.2 million
Gross International Box Office: NA
Total Box Office: $38.2 million+

Story:
This is the movie that made Arnold a star. Arnold's character, Conan, originated in a 1930s comic book called *Weird Tales*. Conan lived on earth in a mythical time called the Hyborian age (12,000 years ago, after the sinking of Atlantis, before historical civilizations), and he and his barbarian tribe were great warriors. In this movie his people fall victim to Thulsa Doom (played by James Earl Jones), leader of a band of raiders who kill everyone in Conan's tribe except the children. The latter are taken as slaves to Doom. Hard labor throughout his childhood on the Wheel of Pain makes Conan a powerful adult, and before long, he becomes a gladiator. His successes lead to his release from captivity, and he vows revenge upon Doom for destroying his family and his people.

The film's producers wanted to make the setting very realistic, so they researched the time period extensively. This prehistoric world was so realistic, they thought, that "an anthropologist can look at this film's culture and say, 'This is consistent.'"[6] Whether that is true or not, Conan had some decidedly modern attitudes toward political power. When Conan and some of his fellow warriors are discussing the things that make life good, Conan declares that living the good life is, "To crush your enemies, see them driven before you, and to hear the lamentation of the women." It was a quote often used against him in the California recall election.

Much of the publicity for this original Conan was about the director, John Milius, a well-know political reactionary who does not like his own culture. His films often depict alternative ways of living, albeit violent and gory ones. Steven Spielberg, his friend, has said that Milius would like to be the heroic figures in his movies. As Milius himself observed of his Conan star, "Arnold is the embodiment of the Superior Man ... There's something wonderfully primeval about him, harking back to the real basic foundational stuff: steel and strength and will."[7]

Title: *Conan the Destroyer*
Release Date: June 29, 1984
Role: Conan, the barbarian, again
Taglines:

- The most powerful legend of all is back in a new adventure.

Gross Domestic Box Office: $26.4 million
Gross International Box Office: NA
Total Box Office: $26.4 million+

Story:

In the inevitable comparison between Conan the Barbarian and Conan the Destroyer, the original Conan was considered a mythic hero while the sequel Conan was called "simply a great hunk of meat, shorn of any emotion or original thought."[8] This Conan was seeking a way to restore life to his lover. His adventure to find the magic potion is filled with more fantastical adventures, people and creatures, seeming more like its comic book source.

But it also focused more on action and less on philosophy. Arnold is quoted in many interviews at the time of the film's release as saying he was asked by the new director, Richard Fleischer, to put on more muscle and to spend most of the film in a loincloth because, as Arnold understood, people wanted to see his body. The film also featured basketball great Wilt Chamberlain as Bombaata, a bodyguard to the Queen.

Title: *Terminator* (aka The Terminator)
Release Date: October 26, 1984
Role: The Terminator, a cyborg assassin
Budget: $6.4 million
Taglines:

- In the Year of Darkness, 2029, the rulers of this planet devised the ultimate plan. They would reshape the Future by changing the Past. The plan required something that felt no pity. No pain. No fear. Something unstoppable. They created "THE TERMINA-TOR."
- The thing that won't die, in the nightmare that won't end.
- Your future is in his hands.

Gross Domestic Box Office: $38.4 million
Gross International Box Office: $42 million
Total Box Office: $80.4 million+

Story:

This is now considered a classic science fiction movie and introduced the character that made Arnold Schwarzenegger even more famous. The Terminator is a cyborg sent from the future to kill the woman, Sarah Connor, who will give birth to a future rebel leader who tries to destroy all the machines, which have taken over the world. Sarah Connor, at this point, is a fluffy waitress with no ambitions and no set future. Terminators, we are told by Kyle Reese, who also comes from the future, are relentless murder machines that can't be reasoned with, can't be bargained with, and cannot be stopped. Reese says, "The Terminator is an infiltration unit, it's part man, part machine. Underneath it's a hyper-alloy combat chassis, microprocessor controlled, fully armored, very tough. But outside it's living human tissue, flesh, skin, hair, blood, grown for the cyborgs." Reese's job is to stop the Terminator from killing Sarah Connor.

The Terminator comes to a police station in search of Sarah Connor. The Terminator enters the police station, and when he is asked to wait for Sarah, he casually surveys the booth the police officer occupies and states without emotion, "I'll be back." He then leaves the building and returns a few seconds later, driving a car into the booth and beginning a violent attack that leaves the police station in tatters. It was one of the few lines he bothers to say in the movie. The original line for the movie was supposed to be, "I'll come back," a statement of the intent to return but without the aggressive tone. It never would have become the same kind of culturally rich phrase that has been repeated millions of times since the movie was first shown. Since then, the phrase "I'll be back" has also been used effectively in each *Terminator* movie, in Arnold's 1987 movie *The Running Man*, and endlessly during the California recall election.

Arnold himself seems to understand why the Terminator appeals to so many people in so many different ways. "Everyone would like to be a Terminator," he has claimed. "Everyone would like to be a person who can take care of the job. Whoever makes you mad, you can get even," he has said in numerous magazine articles and television interviews.[9] He has also said, "I like the Terminator ... I'd like to be as resolved as he was and have that kind of power."[10]

One film critic explained that the movie made Arnold a star because it turned all his "liabilities into perverse virtues: the movie acknowledged his lumbering, robotic quality, and used it as a comic counterpoint to the snappy, quick-witted narrative."[11]

Title: *Red Sonja*
Role: Kalidor, a warrior like Conan, same time, same place
Release Date: July 3, 1985
Budget: $17.9 million

Taglines:

- A woman and a warrior that became a legend

Gross Domestic Box Office: $7 million
Gross International Box Office: NA
Total Box Office: $7 million+

Story:
"It's the worst film I've ever made," Arnold says about this Conan-wannabe movie about a female warrior directed by the same director who made *Conan the Destroyer*. Based again on a comic book story written by the Conan author, Sonja hates men and tries to accomplish her mission of finding a magic talisman without any of their help. Kalidor persists, however, and eventually the two become a sword wielding team.

Box Office, an industry report, asked, "Just how inept is this movie? Well, its cheesy, poorly acted and doesn't make a lot of sense, for starters."[12] It's important to know that at the time these early films of Arnold's came out, no one was being overly optimistic about his chance of becoming a big star. Arnold dated his *Red Sonja* co-star Brigitte Nielsen before she went on to marry Sylvester Stallone.

Title: *Commando*
Role: John Matrix, a retired Army colonel
Release Date: October 4, 1985
Taglines:

- Somewhere … somehow … someone's going to pay!

Gross Domestic Box Office: $35 million
Gross International Box Office: NA
Total Box Office: $35 million+

Story:
Arnold stars as John Matrix, the former head of a special-operations strike force who has retired to a mountain cabin with his daughter Jenny. Jenny is kidnapped by South American bad guys who want Matrix to kill the head of the kidnappers' country and restore a dictator to power. With his usual gusto and wry humor, Arnold goes into the kind of stylized action that one trade magazine described as being like that in a comic book in this basic "exploitation" film.[13]

Following on the *Terminator*, Commando was seen as just another action movie like those of Sylvester Stallone (*Rambo* came out at the same time) or Chuck Norris. One review complained that "the film is mainly designed to show off its star's body and its director's penchant for blowing things up."[14] Arnold claims in a story about the movie that he hopes someday that people will forget about his body, but he knows it is the main asset he has to sell: "I'm a businessman. I'm interested in the movie making money. I'm not hung up on being an actor's actor or doing what they call artistic movies."[15]

Arnold comments in his Web site that he did all his own stunts in this movie, but in the future it would be easier to just use a computer generated version of him. But as always, emphasizing his unique size, he comments, "But I don't think they have a big enough computer yet. What is it, a gigabyte? With these muscles, you're going to need a lot of those."[16]

Title: *Raw Deal*

Role: Mark Kaminski (also spelled Kaminsky), an ex-FBI agent
Release Date: June 6, 1986
Taglines:

- The government gave him a raw deal. Nobody gives him a raw deal.
- Nobody gives him a Raw Deal.
- His trigger has all the answers.
- The system gave him a raw deal. Nobody gives him a raw deal.

Gross Domestic Box Office: $16.2 million
Gross International Box Office: NA
Total Box Office: $16.2 million+

Story:
The raw deal in this story refers to the sacking of FBI agent Mark Kaminski for use of excess force. He becomes a southern sheriff and seems content but then is asked to infiltrate the Chicago mob to get himself reinstated. Getting accepted by the mob, he eventually gets discovered and has to perform a major bloodbath to escape and end the story without any immoral actions (except killing lots of people) and with no doubts about his righteousness.

The production notes used to advertise the film claimed that Arnold had expanded as an actor after the *Terminator* role. With the release of this movie, however, critics were still baffled by how Arnold can be considered an actor when it is still nearly impossible to understand him. The *New Yorker*, in its review, joked, "He speaks in a weird soft rumble, as if he had built up the muscles in his mouth, too, and couldn't get English words past them."[17]

Title: *Predator*
Role: Major Alan "Dutch" Schaeffer (sometimes spelled Schaefer)
Release Date: June 12, 1987
Budget: $18 million
Taglines:

- Nothing like it has ever been on earth before.
- It came for the thrill of the hunt. It picked the wrong man to hunt.
- Soon the hunt will begin.
- Nothing like it has ever been on Earth before. It came from another planet for the thrill of the hunt. It picked the wrong man.
- In a part of the world where there are no rules, deep in the jungle where nothing that lives is safe, an elite rescue squad is being led by the ultimate warrior. But now, they're up against the ultimate enemy. Nothing like it has ever been on earth before. It kills for pleasure, it hunts for sport. But this time, it picked the wrong man to hunt.
- We cannot see it, but it sees the heat of our bodies and the heat of our fear.
- In this movie, Arnold will experience every meaning of the word " Pain."

Gross Domestic Box Office: $59.7
Gross International Box Office: NA
Total Box Office: $59.7 million+

Story:
Arnold plays the well-respected leader of a commando unit that is commissioned to go to an unnamed Central or South American country to rescue a kidnapped hostage and a team of soldiers already sent and lost. What they encounter in a dense and dangerous jungle instead is a huge alien creator that has killed and skinned their comrades and now threatens them.

The *Predator* that is stalking them is an alien bigger than Arnold and equipped with special vision, cloaking capabilities, and great strength. It seems to take delight in hunting humans as if in a game. In fact, *Predator* became a convincing computer/video game soon after its release with early versions showing up on the Commodore

Amiga and the Commodore 64 in 1989. You can now play a *Predator* game on your mobile phone.

Roger Ebert of the *Chicago Sun-Times* gave the movie a positive review despite the lack of logic in its storyline. He comments: "And the action moves so quickly that we overlook questions such as (1) Why would an alien species go to all the effort to send a creature to Earth, just so that it could swing from trees and skin American soldiers? Or, (2) Why would a creature so technologically advanced need to bother with hand-to-hand combat, when it could just zap Arnold with a ray gun?"[18]

The final battle pits Arnold's all too human body against the technologically superior alien who takes off part of his body armor to battle the soft-bodied, although muscular, human. Arnold wins by tricking the beast, who seems to get tripped up by his own arrogance. The film also featured wrestler Jesse "The Body" Ventura, who went on to become governor of Minnesota before Arnold was elected in California.

Title: *The Running Man*
Role: Ben Richards, a helicopter pilot with the federal police
Release Date: November 13, 1987
Budget: $27 million
Taglines:

- A game nobody survives. But Schwarzenegger has yet to play.
- It is the year 2017. "The Running Man" is a deadly game no one has ever survived. But … Schwarzenegger has yet to play.
- 2019. A game nobody survives. This year might be the exception.

Gross Domestic Box Office: $38.1 million
Gross International Box Office: NA
Total Box Office: $38.1 million+

Story:
This story is set in the near future (both the years 2017 and 2019 appear in reviews and ads) in post-quake California, and America has become a fascist state. Arnold's character Ben Richards works for the government and is ordered to shoot at people rioting for food in California. When he refuses, someone else butchers 1,500 innocent citizens, and Richards gets blamed.

Unfortunately for him, the government runs a popular reality television program that takes criminals like him and puts them through a series of televised games where they are stalked and usually killed. Richards, announcing before he is sent off to face the deadly Stalkers, "I'll be back," is actually successful fending off his killers. In typical Arnold fashion, he makes jokes as he commits mayhem, saying, "He had to split," of a man he cut in half with a saw, and "He was a real pain in the neck," about a man he strangles.

This movie anticipated the reality television craze in the United States by a decade. Reality TV uses common people, supposedly unscripted scenarios, and various embarrassing or challenging situations to create entertainment. There has always been some element of reality TV, especially through game shows and talk shows, but it really developed its widespread popularity with the introduction of *American Idol* (2002), *Survivor* (2000) and one of the earliest, MTV's *The Real World* (1992).

Title: *Red Heat*
Role: Ivan Danko, a Soviet cop
Release Date: June 14, 1988
Taglines:

> • Moscow's toughest detective. Chicago's craziest cop. There's only one thing worse than making them mad. Making them partners.

Gross Domestic Box Office: $35 million
Gross International Box Office: NA
Total Box Office: $35 million+

Story:
Arnold's Web site claims this movie is a "high-action character study," but to most critics it looked like a typical Schwarzenegger film designed to please fans of unimaginative action films. Arnold plays Ivan Danko, a Soviet police captain who comes to Chicago to extradite a drug lord back to the Soviet Union. Danko is out of his element, not understanding the restraint and rules of the American system. The humor is in the physical and intellectual contrast between Arnold and the American cop, Art Ridzik, played by Jim Belushi. *The New York Times* dismissed it as "a topically entertaining variation on the sort of action-adventure nonsense that plays best on television."[19]

Director Walter Hill makes no apologies for making a strict genre film that gives the audience what they expect but may not please the intellectuals. In the classic buddy movie mold, Danko and Ridzik are opposites and have to learn to like and help each other. But the story didn't work for some critics, and the characters had no charisma and were "… dull unlikable noodleheads" who participate in "garden-variety cop stuff: high-speed chases and bloody shoot-outs."[20]

Title: *Twins*
Role: Julius Benedict, an experiment in human genetics
Release Date: December 8, 1988
Budget: $15 million
Taglines:

- Only their mother can tell them apart.
- Inconceivable! Pregnant? Hard to believe! Twins? It's obvious!

Gross Domestic Box Office: $112 million
Gross International Box Office: $105 million
Total Box Office: $217 million+

Story:
This is the first film that featured Arnold in a comedy role. It is also one of the first indications of the extent of his deal making success in Hollywood. Instead of being paid his usual $10 million salary, Arnold opted for a percentage of the ticket sales, initially 15%, but that rose with the increase in sales. He made well over $10 million because the film was a huge success.

The story and the premise of the film are odd, but the uniqueness is one of its selling points. Arnold plays Julius Benedict, a product of genetic experiments conducted by the American government. The goal of the experiment was the production of a physically, mentally and spiritually advanced human being. Julius had not one but six genetically excellent fathers, and his mother was an Aryan beauty who supposedly died giving birth. Later he discovers his mother is alive.

Much to Julius' surprise, he also discovers that he has a twin brother, Vincent, played by Danny DeVito. DeVito's character is a short, balding rascal who steals cars and seduces married women. Julius, on the other hand, is the perfect human specimen who claims to hate violence, can speak twelve languages, and is still inexperienced with women. The genetic scientist who attempted to produce this perfect man, Julius, explains to the two brothers that when their embryo split in two, it did not split equally. All the purity and strength and quality went to Julius, and all the "crap that was left over" went into Vincent, the "side-effect" who was just "genetic trash."

The humor is immediate when you see DeVito and Arnold side-by-side: one very short and round, the other tall and muscular. The story promotes the idea that the two men, despite their differences, need each other, so they can learn about the other half of life. They end up becoming business partners, marry sisters, and each ends up having a set of twins. The film received mixed critical reviews, but audiences made the movie a hit. The role left an enduring image, and Arnold claims on his Web site that the kids who acted in *Kindergarten Cop* with him asked where Danny DeVito, his twin brother was.[21]

Title: *Total Recall*
Role: Doug Quaid, a construction worker and Hauser, a government secret agent
Release Date: June 1, 1990
Budget: $65 million+
Taglines:

- They stole his mind, now he wants it back.
- Get ready for the ride of your life.
- What would you do if someone stole your mind?

Gross Domestic Box Office: $119.4 million
Gross International Box Office: $142 million
Total Box Office: $261.4 million+

Story:
After his comedy role in *Twins*, Arnold turned to an exciting adventure story he had been trying to get made for years. It became the most expensive film made to that date. *Total Recall* is the story of a civil war on the planet Mars in the year 2084 and is based on a story by famed science fiction writer Philip K. Dick. In this futuristic tale, Arnold is a construction worker who has a desire to go to Mars and dreams endlessly and vividly of his possible adventures there.

Since his wife is opposed to an actual vacation trip there, he goes to a company called Rekall, Inc., which implants manufactured memories of fabulous vacations. While the memory of a vacation to Mars is being implanted, a hidden memory is discovered, and it turns out that Quaid is really a secret agent, Hauser, and really has been to Mars. He goes there to try to find out his true identity. The task is not that simple, and Quaid/Hauser gets caught up in the rebellion that the Mars community is developing to protest their lack of food, water, and oxygen. He finds the woman who has appeared in his dreams, and together they uncover a tyrannical plot to control Mars.

Critics still have trouble with Arnold as an actor at this point. Some continue to complain about his mangling of the English language, and others think his body still gets in the way of taking him seriously as an actor. One wrote, "Try as he might, Arnold is ... well, Arnold ... Arnold remains the same lumbering, if likable, lug. Once he opens his mouth to recite any dialogue, smart or dumb, its Hans and Franz time again."[22] Many still look back at the *Terminator* as Arnold's best role: "*Total Recall* is so terrible that it wipes out our last, stubbornest images of brief pleasure Schwarzenegger gave us when he played an automaton. We may even believe that *The Terminator* never really happened—that it was just some kind of brain implant. A trick designed to lure us, again and again, into a dark room where a giant will knock us senseless and take our money."[23]

Title: *Kindergarten Cop*
Role; John Kimble, Los Angeles cop and undercover kindergarten teacher
Release Date: December 21, 1990
Budget: $15 million
Taglines:

- An undercover cop in a class by himself.
- Go ahead, you tell him you didn't do your homework.
- He's the toughest undercover cop in LA. If you're bad, he'll know it. If you're hiding something, he'll find out. If you cheat, he can tell. Now ... Go ahead, *you* tell him you didn't do your homework.
- It's a jungle gym out there.

Gross Domestic Box Office: $91.5 million
Gross International Box Office: $110.5 million
Total Box Office: $202 million+

Story:
Kindergarten Cop is depicted in a multi-page spread in *The Saturday Evening Post* as a gentle comedy that features Arnold as a cop who becomes a kindergarten teacher to conduct an undercover drug

investigation. Emphasizing the supposed change of focus in Arnold's roles "from muscle to mirth," the review ignores the fact that this is one of the most graphically violent films Arnold has ever made.[24] It trades in the comic book, abstract violence of endlessly exploding vehicles and long distance gunnings for upclose shootings and beatings. One group of kids in Oregon who acted as extras in the film were not allowed to see it by their teachers, who had to cancel a field trip to the theatre after one teacher reported it had excessive sex, violence, and vulgarity.[25]

Arnold is Los Angeles detective John Kimble, who has been tracking a drug lord for four years. He needs the man's wife to testify against, him but she has disappeared along with the man's young son. Kimble has to get to them first and goes to an Oregon town to try to identify them. He goes undercover as a kindergarten teacher after his female partner, who was supposed to take the job, got food poisoning.

The humor is in watching the big muscled Arnold get completely overwhelmed by a room full of frisky, energetic and decidedly disobedient 5-year-olds. After losing his cool, Mr. Kimble returns to class with a plan. Because the kids "lack discipline," he is going to impose it on their once carefree lives. In another odd take on Arnold's screen persona, the classroom becomes like a fascist boot camp, and the children are shown as progressively happier as they give up their messy, immature ways. It is an odd take on children, described by one reviewer as, "It's like watching the Terminator host *Sesame Street*."

Arnold's comic adventures as a teacher are wedged in the middle of the film and as the *Los Angeles Times* explained, we are meant to accept that this is a "kinder, gentler" Arnold.[26] These are the same words used by then President George H.W. Bush, who was elected in 1988 on the promise to build a kinder, gentler nation. The *Times* article concludes that the entire purpose of the film is to "show what a swell guy Kimble-Schwarzenegger is becoming."[27]

Title: *Terminator 2: Judgment Day*
Release Date: July 1, 1991
Budget: $100 million
Taglines:

- Ten Years Ago. The Machines Who Rule the Future Sent An Unstoppable Terminator to Assassinate the Yet Unborn John Connor. They Failed. In 1991, the Machines Will Try Again.
- It's nothing personal.
- This time there are two.
- Same Make. Same Model. New Mission.

Gross Domestic Box Office: $205 million
Gross International Box Office: $312 million
Total Box Office: $517 million+

Story:
Sarah Connor has escaped the Terminator in the first film, crushing him in a machine and leaving only his metallic arm intact. But that arm, as we learn at the end of this film, is what will cause Judgment Day, the destruction of humans and the rise of the machines, because scientists will study it and make the sentient machines that will eventually take over the world.

Sarah Connor has been preparing for this. After the birth of her son John, the future leader of the rebellion, Sarah learned all she could about combat and about what was happening with the machines. When we first see Sarah in T2, she is no longer the delicate and demure girl from the first movie. She is now a pumped and cut fighting machine, a fierce and angry woman whose mission to save the world has gotten her locked up in a mental hospital.

This time there are two terminators: the original one played again by Arnold has been reprogrammed to help Sarah and John Connor instead of destroy them. The evil terminator this time is the T-1000, a liquid metal, "mimetic polyalloy" shapeshifter, which means it can imitate almost anything. It could even be argued that there is a third terminator, Sarah, who abandons any sort of motherly role and enters combat with frightful intensity.

The recasting of Arnold's terminator as a good guy was a brilliant marketing strategy. Making the Terminator's destructive habits focused on an evil cyborg rather than a mother and her child opens up the possibility of seeing him as a hero and eventually as a cultural icon who could be used as a metaphor for any number of big, violent, aggressive things. Arnold was firmly morphed into the Terminator through this movie more than the first.

Sarah is guided by a saying that is supposed to be message from their future son John: "The future is not set. There is no fate but what we make for ourselves." It could be Arnold Schwarzenegger speaking about his own life.

Title: *Last Action Hero*
Role: Jack Slater, an action hero in the movies, and Arnold Schwarzenegger as himself
Release Date: June 18, 1993

Budget: $85 million

Taglines:

- This isn't the movies anymore.

Gross Domestic Box Office: $50 million

Gross International Box Office: $71 million

Total Box Office: $121 million+

Story:

If we were to pick one movie that could illuminate Arnold's career as a cinema hero, it wouldn't be the Terminator films or Conan, it would be this turkey. The movie is an oddball attempt to be self-conscious about the relationship between movies and reality. It ended up becoming one of Hollywood's huge flops and a case study of misreading both the market and Arnold's appeal. It made only $15 million its opening weekend; besides its hefty production budget, it had cost at least $30 million to advertise.

Of a test screening that panicked the films' producers weeks before the movie came out, one attendee said, "The movie lay there like a big fried egg."[28] The studio that produced the film attempted to blame the press for the bad reception of the film, or the popularity of *Jurassic Park*, which had opened a week earlier, but the fact is that this is one very confused and unpleasant film. The film was supposed to be advertised on the outside of an actual rocket that was being launched into space, but the rocket never left the launch pad.

Last Action Hero is the story of a boy, Danny, who loves the movies. His favorite star is Jack Slater, an action movie hero. The boy gets a magic ticket that lets him enter the world behind the screen, and he has all the fantasy adventures that take place in the movies. Some evil guys get a hold of the ticket and enter the real world, so Jack and Danny follow to make sure they get sent back to the world of fantasy. The mix of comedy and action that was supposed to make this movie appeal to several audiences ended up driving both types away. The publicity package for the film claimed somewhat hopefully, "Slater learns that even though he is a fictional hero, he actually enriches people's lives."

In many ways, *The Last Action Hero* documents what Arnold would have become without the Terminator's success as Arnold's alter ego. In the movie, the character Slater is asked by Danny to say the phrase "I'll be back." Slater doesn't know what he is talking about (because of course the character Slater is neither the Terminator nor Arnold Schwarzenegger), but the boy insists that, "Everybody waits for you to keep working it in. It's kind of like your calling card." Slater refuses. In *The Last Action Hero*, the character of Jack Slater never says that line. Instead, the director of *The Last Action Hero* ironically chose to have Sylvester Stallone pictured in a *Terminator 2* film poster, astride a motorcycle with the famous leather and shades outfit. *The Last Action Hero* shows Slater's action movies as increasingly repetitive and occupied by unbelievable components like a cartoon rabbit, screaming bosses, incompetent police officers, and incredibly gorgeous women everywhere. It also shows Slater as wanting a better connection to his family and as not being able to tell real life from screen life. In some ways, it illustrates what really happened to Sylvester Stallone's career, not Schwarzenegger's.

The violence in the movie was kept out of the advertisements at first, but after its first unsuccessful weekend, the action and violence aspects were introduced in new ads. It didn't work, and the toys associated with the movie also flopped. Arnold was trying to answer criticisms about the excess violence in his films by making one that emphasized other things, but as one Hollywood insider complained about the Jack Slater action figures that had no weapons, "You know what an action figure without a gun is? It's a *doll*."[29] Arnold, Hollywood's sure thing, had just flopped.

Title: *True Lies*
Role: Harry Tasker, computer salesman and secret spy
Release Date: July 15, 1994
Budget: $120 million
Taglines:

- When he said I do, he never said what he did.

Gross Domestic Box Office: $146 million
Gross International Box Office: $219 million
Total Box Office: $365 million+

Story:
As recently as October, 2005, rumors that Arnold was planning to star in the sequel to *True Lies*, called *True Lies 2*, were competing with the daily reports of the mundane work of the governor of California. The first movie was very financially rewarding for Arnold, who earned a large salary and a percentage of the profits.

The first *True Lies* was, again, reported to be the most expensive movie made to that point. Coming out in the late summer against *The Lion King* ($783 million worldwide) and *Forrest Gump* ($679.4 million worldwide), *True Lies* nevertheless went on to earn more than $365 million.

Like *Twins* and *Kindergarten Cop*, *True Lies* was a high-concept film that was designed to play off expectations of what Arnold could and couldn't do, especially, again, because of his accent. As one film reviewer joked, the story would seem to have "a built-in credibility problem for a man with Arnold's accent, since a man with Arnold's accent could only be one of three things: a robot with a faulty voice program, an ex-weightlifter who can't act but becomes an overpaid movie star, or a spy, and who would believe the first two?"[30]

The film ended up being described in many different ways, perhaps to fend off the confusion of Arnold's last film, *Last Action Hero*. But the claim on Arnold's Web site that it was an "action-adventure-comedy-romance-thriller" or the executive producer's claim that it was a "domestic epic" were not the factors responsible for making this a huge international hit. This story of a man whose family thinks he is a boring computer salesman but who is really a suave, action-oriented spy earned Arnold a $15 million salary plus points. Director James Cameron said that after Arnold's last disaster, the idea was to "charge ahead and leave them in the dust."[31] The film was released two weeks later than expected, but its opening coordinated with Arnold putting his hand and foot prints in the cement at Mann's Chinese Theater in Hollywood.

Harry Tasker, the man who lied to his wife and family for 17 years about his real job, had a surprise in store. His bored nerdy secretary wife Helen decides to spice up her own life by considering an affair with a car salesman, who, just coincidently, was pretending to be a secret agent. When Harry finds out, he arranges a pretend adventure for Helen to make her feel wanted, but the two end up having to fight real terrorists (Arabs, of course, and real protests by Arab Americans followed) who have nuclear weapons. The outrageous scenarios the two have to survive and the revved up machinery they use to do it are the work of *Terminator*'s James Cameron, who simply confirms his identity as a "fearless and free-spending ultra-macho perfectionist."[32]

Reactions to Helen's character was mixed, especially because in addition to her heroics, she is humiliated by her husband when she performs a striptease that her husband tricks her into thinking is necessary for catching a spy. Others thought it was insensitive given all the publicity in Los Angeles over the brutal murder of O. J. Simpson's ex-wife just a month earlier.[33] Another reviewer noted that despite his reputation for offering powerful women characters, James Cameron is no fool and "knows exactly which way the political winds are blowing,"[34] presumably meaning powerful women are now out of style. That reviewer concluded, "When Tasker's sidekick, Gib (Tom Arnold), cackles, 'Women—can't live with 'em, can't kill 'em,' it's a sick little twist on pop-culture vernacular. At the moment [i.e., after the Simpson murders], however, the joke is nothing less than bone-chilling."[35]

Title: *Junior*
Role: Dr. Alex Hesse
Release Date: November 23, 1994
Taglines:

• Nothing is inconceivable.

Gross Domestic Box Office: $36 million
Gross International Box Office: $54 million
Total Box Office: $90 million+

Story:
Arnold explains on his Web site that being one of the biggest stars in Hollywood gave him the freedom to do any kind of movie he wanted. But his decision to make a movie in which he was the first man to get pregnant and deliver a baby was widely ridiculed as, if not an abuse of that freedom, then at least a really bad decision.

Arnold plays Alex Hesse, described in the production information packet as a "brilliant but fiercely disciplined scientist."[36] He has been working with the unorthodox gynecologist Larry Arbogast, played by Danny DeVito, to get approval for a drug called "Expectane," which will help take pregnancies to full term. When their drug testing is halted, they take samples of the drug and a fertilized embryo. They implant the embryo in Dr. Hesse's abdomen and give him doses of the drug, making him the first successfully pregnant man.

Unexpectedly, Hesse wants to keep the pregnancy going. Director Ivan Reitman explains in the production notes that he wants to "take Arnold Schwarzenegger, an icon of masculinity, and see what happens when he has to deal with one of the great events of life heretofore reserved for women—giving birth."[37] Arnold later appointed Reitman to his transition team when he was elected governor.

In a stereotype of pregnant women, Hesse becomes more and more emotional. When Arbogast finds out about the pregnancy, the two have to hide this information and end up (again) as an odd couple until the delivery. Complicating matters is the arrival of researcher Diana Reddin, played by Emma Thompson, with whom Dr. Hesse develops a romantic relationship. By the end of the movie, all the more traditional male-female couplings are restored, and there are babies all around with the women, this time, doing the delivering.

Arnold claimed in hindsight that he made this "heartwarming" story about motherhood to honor his wife Maria and the experiences she had bringing three children (at that time) into the world.[38] Maria Shriver appeared on the *Tonight Show* some months after one of her pregnancies and explained how Arnold himself taught her what to do in the delivery room. She explained how their birthing coach took a doll and, after instructing Arnold to put his legs up in the birthing position, put the doll between his legs and yelled at him to push. Maria demonstrated Arnold pushing and breathing hard and delivering the baby doll. Maria then commented, "Arnold delivered the little baby and I watched him and knew what to do. That's how I learned how to give birth."

Talking about Arnold's stereotypical behavior as a whiny, sentimental pregnant woman, Kenneth Turan asked, "If it's no longer acceptable for white folks to don makeup and mimic black behavior, or for males to prance around being clichéd, limp-wristed gays, it is an interesting question why this kind of comedy remains more than acceptable."[39] Turan is wrong, of course, because all of those depictions are clearly still acceptable comic forms in many parts of the culture.

Not all critics minded the movie, finding it a farce worth watching, but audiences didn't buy it at all. Whether the problem was that Arnold was once again changing his screen image, this time in a big way, or that the idea itself may have sounded funny to Hollywood producers but not to Arnold's fans, audiences stayed away from this 1994 holiday release.

Title: *Eraser*
Role: John Kruger, a U.S. Marshall working for witness protection
Release Date: June 11, 1996
Budget: $100 million

Taglines:

- He will erase your past to protect your future.

Gross Domestic Box Office: $101.3 million
Gross International Box Office: $133.8 million
Total Box Office: $235.1 million+

Story:
Arnold plays John "The Eraser" Kruger, an extremely efficient U.S. marshal who helps endangered citizens enter the federal witness protection program. His job is to eliminate all traces of these people's previous identities. His newest charge is Dr. Lee Cullen (Vanessa Williams) who has to hide because of information she has about illegal business dealings. Vanessa Williams later sang the national anthem at Arnold's inaugural.

On his Web site, Arnold describes his fascination with the ideas in this movie: "I'd always been incredibly fascinated about the idea of the witness protection program … how people's identities can just be erased and they can end up in different parts of the world, with different papers, different backgrounds … the real you doesn't exist anymore."[40] It is very much the trajectory Arnold has taken in his movies, with varied success. This film had a rocky road in its production with enormous cost overruns and a lack or organization.

Its reviews were mixed, and its domestic box office barely paid the bills, and it left little impression on the cultural landscape. By now, reviews of Arnold's films complained less about his acting or his speech and concentrated on the quality and quantity of explosions and weapons. It's an amazing change in the critical landscape and points as much to Schwarzenegger's great weight in the industry, as it does to an inability to distinguish all the similarly themed action movies Arnold made between his signature Terminator films.

Title: *Jingle All the Way*
Role: Howard Langston,
Release Date: November 22, 1996
Budget: $60 million
Taglines:

- Two Dads, One Toy, No Prisoners

Gross Domestic Box Office: $60.5 million
Gross International Box Office: $65.1 million
Total Box Office: $125.6 million+

Story:
Arnold earned $20 million for this holiday story that was promoted as a PG "family film" but that has a nasty undertone and more than its share of violence. Once again the film seems to barely break even in domestic sales, yet Arnold continues to be offered films that bank on his popularity.

Arnold plays a harried father, Howard Langston, in Minnesota who neglects his family responsibilities. When he doesn't show up for one of his son's karate class awards ceremonies, he promises the boy anything he wants for Christmas. The boy picks a "Turboman," the most sought after action figure that year, but Howard forgets to buy it, and on Christmas Eve he has to battle dozens of other last-minute parents looking for the same thing. Sinbad plays another somewhat crazy father who relentlessly appears at all the same places Howard does to find one of the figures. The obsession for the toy escalates and becomes an excuse for all sorts of mayhem, disconnected slapstick and a too-neat ending.

Title: *Batman and Robin*
Role: Mr. Freeze/Dr. Victor Fries
Release Date: June 12, 1997
Budget: $125 million
Taglines:

- Strength. Courage. Honor. And loyalty. On June 20, it ALL comes together …

Gross Domestic Box Office: $107.3 million
Gross International Box Office: $130 million
Total Box Office: $237.3 million+

Story:
Arnold's salary alone was $25 million and that for this film in which he is not even the main character. Arnold steps into this fourth movie in the Batman series as the latest threat to Batman, Robin, and Gotham City. He is Mr. Freeze, who threatens to freeze over the entire city and then the world. This Nobel prize-winning biochemist is peeved with humanity because he failed to cure his wife's dreaded disease and messed up his metabolism in the process, making him one cold guy. He wears an armored suit that keeps his body cold and has cool weapons that can freeze his enemies on contact. He has to steal diamonds to keep his personal refrigerator going.

The film is so ludicrous, one reviewer wrote, that Arnold delivers what should be his most villainous lines "in such a bored, detached way, that he sounds less like a super-villain ordering a massacre, and more like a gas station attendant giving a motorist directions to the Interstate." [41] Arnold might want to heed Mr. Freeze's warning: "Allow me to break the ice. My name is Freeze. Learn it well. For it's the chilling sound of your doom."

Just four months before the release of this movie, Arnold underwent elective heart surgery to repair a damaged valve. He was back in action in time to help promote the film when it was released. Arnold credits the movie experience with increasing his knowledge of movie marketing because the Batman franchise has a wide-ranging merchandising machine associated with it.

On the Website "the four word film review," where contributors have to give an analysis of a movie in no more than four words, the following contributions describe *Batman and Robin:*[42]

Ahnuld gives frozen performance.
Arnie freezes franchise.
Schwarzenegger combats global warming.
Freeze fits stiff Schwarzenegger.
Batman series's quality: TERMINATED!
Arnold Schwarzenegger, career freeze.
Arnold makes ice jokes.

Title: *End of Days*
Role: Jericho Cane
Release Date: November 24, 1999
Budget: $83 million
Taglines:

- Prepare for the end.
- The end is near
- When the thousand years are expired, Satan shall be loosed out of his prison.
- Prepare for the end of days.
- On the eve of the millennium, an ex-cop torn by loss must regain his faith to quell the end of days.
- You will bear witness to the End of Days …

Gross Domestic Box Office: $66.9 million
Gross International Box Office: $142.4 million
Total Box Office: $209.3 million+

Story:

Are you keeping track? Another $25 million went to Arnold for this end of the millennium story about the Devil's return to earth at the turn of the century to father a child with a chosen female. It may be hard to remember that the end of the millennium was causing great fear, but not because the Devil was about looking for his girl. It had more to do with potential computer glitches, but that is not a plot-line that fits with Arnold's style.

This is the first film Arnold made since his heart surgery two and a half years earlier and the slowed-down Jericho Cane reflects that. Maybe the appeal was that director Peter Hyams attitude was that, "This is as pro-religious a movie as you can make."[43]

Arnold plays Cane, an ex-cop turned security guard who has lost his family and is bitter and depressed and maybe even suicidal. He gets involved with the scheme that the Devil has planned for New Year's Eve and has to find a new way to defeat Satan so the world will not be plunged into darkness. If it were 20 years earlier, one reviewer writes, "[O]ne can even imagine being thrilled by what would have seemed like wickedly irrelevant dialogue, breath-taking action and mind-boggling special effects."[44] But that era is gone and the twenty-first century requires more to keep its jaded audiences going.

Title: *The 6th Day*
Role: Adam Gibson, a helicopter pilot
Release Date: November 13, 2000
Budget: $82 million
Taglines:

- Are You Ready!
- Are You Who You Think You Are?
- You've cloned the wrong man.
- I might be back.
- I know who I am.
- They picked the wrong man to clone.

Gross Domestic Box Office: $34.5 milliion
Gross International Box Office: $67 million
Total Box Office: $101.5 million+

Story:

Arnold's movies have often been slightly ahead of the curve, anticipating or predicting things that were about to become important in the culture. This was one of those movies with its plot about human and animal cloning. In *The 6th Day*, Arnold is Adam Gibson, who comes home from a near fatal helicopter crash for his birthday party only to find that he has been cloned, and his duplicate is now enjoying his party, his family, and his life. Gibson has to find out what is going on and who is behind this mess and has to dodge his enemies who find out he survived.

Critics were not kind to this movie with one saying, "The film's subject is appropriate because almost everything in the movie seems to be lifted from the DNA of other pictures. Despite some deft touches, this logy thriller seems so familiar that you may find yourself waiting for its star, Arnold Schwarzenegger, to awake and find that he's actually in *Total Recall*. While the cloning plot has potential, the same reviewer noted that, 'Science can clone Adam, but it can't create a double whose accent is easier to understand.' "[45]

Arnold did not have the same hesitations about cloning that Adam Gibson did. Arnold told *Muscle & Fitness* magazine after the movie came out, "I never worried about cloning; as a matter of fact, at times I've wished I could clone myself because there are so many ambitions and so many goals in my life, and there's not enough time to do all those things."[46] On his Web site he explains it as, "I think it would be great to be cloned. One of me could do films, another could spend time with Maria and my family, and the other could spend the rest of the time on the golf course."[47]

Title: *Collateral Damage*
Role: Gordy Brewer, a fireman in Los Angeles
Release Date: February 4, 2002
Budget: $85 million
Taglines:

- What Would You Do If You Lost Everything?
- Nothing is more dangerous than a man with nothing to lose.

Gross Domestic Box Office: $40 million
Gross International Box Office: $38.3 million
Total Box Office: $78.3 million+

Story:
Collateral Damage, as a new Arnold Schwarzenegger film about to be released on October 5, 2001, was hardly noticed before the September 11 attacks on New York, Washington, and Pennsylvania.

The film, which is the story of a fireman seeking revenge for the death of his family from a terrorist attack, was actually being advertised on large billboards in Manhattan when the attacks occurred. After the attacks, which were often described as looking like disaster movies, the producers of *Collateral Damage* withdrew the film. At first the word was that it would never come out, but eventually Warner Brothers released it on February 4, 2002.

After the film's release, it was impossible to review it without mentioning its initial release date, as well as the similarities between the movie and real events. Elvis Mitchell, in the *New York Times*, saw it as a rehash of past Schwarzenegger films and a sad commentary on Arnold's career: "[A]s Mr. Schwarzenegger's stature as an action figure diminishes, his effort to retain a piece of the market is touching."[48] Other reviews were worse. The *San Francisco Chronicle* said, "In other words, *Collateral Damage* is trash, but it earns extra points by acting as if it weren't."[49] And the *Village Voice* points out the obvious issue that caused numerous media outlets to pay attention to an otherwise mundane movie: "An embarrassment on September 12, a patriotic vision five months later."[50]

Title: *Terminator 3: The Rise of the Machines*
Role: The Terminator
Release Date: July 2, 2003
Budget: $175 million
Taglines:

• The Machines Will Rise.

Gross Domestic Box Office: $150.3 million
Gross International Box Office: $267.9 million
Total Box Office: $418.2 million+

Story:
This was the last film released before Arnold ran for governor of California. It was a huge hit, although it continued the pattern of not having the U.S. box office even cover the cost of having the film made. The international box office was necessary for the film to show a profit. Arnold earned a base salary of $30 million.

The movie continues the story of John Connor and his attempts to keep a low profile, so he isn't eliminated by the terminators from the future. The latest terminator is an even more sophisticated version of the T-1000, a mimetic polyalloy that can change shapes. This one takes on the image of a sexy blonde woman with a determined stare and adaptable weaponry. It is called a T-X or Terminatrix.

John and his future wife Kate are the targets this time, and it also turns out that Kate's father is the one responsible for unleashing the machines in the first place when he puts the Skynet protocols into effect. At the end of *Terminator 3*, a nuclear war has been launched by SkyNet, a computer network that had been made so sophisticated it has become "aware of itself." The computer program has effectively terminated humanity's ability to control communication, defense, and all the other necessities of life. The network has determined that humans are unfit. John and Kate escape with the help of Arnold's friendly terminator. They hide in a mountain bunker designed to protect the American leaders in the event of just such nuclear destruction. But, with typical human failure, the leaders were caught unawares, and they never make it to safety. John and Kate will form the core of the resistance.

By the time the movie came out, there was already much speculation that Arnold would run for governor. Like *Collateral Damage*, this movie got caught up with real events, but in the case of T3, the results were more profitable. A. O. Scott says in the *New York Times* that Arnold "acts (if you can call it that) with his usual leaden whimsy, manifesting the gift for uttering hard-to-forget, meaningless catch phrases that is most likely the wellspring of his blossoming reported desire to seek elective office in California.[51] *USA Today* commented that, "The question isn't just whether it was worth the 12-year wait [since T2]. It's also whether T3 will hasten star Arnold Schwarzenegger's entry into politics. It could."[52]

Title: *Around the World in 80 Days*
Role: Prince Hapi
Release Date: June 16, 2004
Budget: $110 million
Taglines:

- The race begins: June 16.
- Let your imagination soar.

Gross Domestic Box Office: $24 million
Gross International Box Office:$42.5 million
Total Box Office: $66.5 million

Story:

The last of Governor Schwarzenegger's films to actually be released features Arnold in only a very small role. It was a bigger failure than most of his own recent films. The story is from the classic novel that finds inventor Phileas Fogg and his traveling companion Passepartout as they try to win a bet that takes them around the world. Arnold plays the Turkish Prince Hapi, who hosts the travelers as they pass through. With his odd wig and goofy grin, he seems like a cartoon character. Film critic Roger Ebert liked Arnold in this movie: "The California governor's scenes were shot before he took office, and arguably represent his last appearance in a fiction film; if so, he leaves the movies as he entered, a man who shares our amusement at his improbability, and has a canny sense of his own image and possibilities."[53]

NOTES

1. Brian Lowry, "Schwarzenegger adds body to his acting as 'Conan The Barbarian,'" *UCLA Bruin*, April 28, 1982, p. 21.

2. All box office figures and budget figures are from IMDbPro.com and are often confirmed in other sources. But keep in mind that these figures, because of the complexities of Hollywood financing, are never completely divulged to the public.

3. See "user comments" on IMDb, http://proimdb.com/title/tt0065832/usercomments.

4. Studs Terkel, *American Dreams: Lost and Found* (New York: Ballantine Books, 1980), pp. 140–142.

5. See http://www.dvdverdict.com/reviews/thevillain.shtml.

6. Kirk Honeycut, "Milius the Barbarian," *American Film*, May 1982, p. 34.

7. Bill Zehme, "Mr. Big Shot," *Rolling Stone*, August 22, 1991, p. 41.

8. Derek Elley, "Review: Conan the Destroyer," *Films and Filming*, 1984, p. 37.

9. Zehme, "Mr. Big Shot," p. 42.

10. K. W. Woods, *Schwarzenegger: Muscleman to Terminator (An Unauthorized Biography)* (Lincolnwood, IL: Publications International, 1991), p. 6.

11. Terence Rafferty, "Terminated," *The New Yorker*, June 18, 1990, p. 51.

12. *Box Office*, September 1985, R-113.

13. *Box Office*, December 1985, R-137.

14. Kim Newman, *Monthly Film Bulletin*, February 1986, p. 42.

15. Gerald Clarke, "New Muscle at the Box Office," *Time*, October 28, 1985. Accessed online (requires registration), http://www.time.com/time/archive/preview/0,10987,960242,00.html.

16. See http://www.schwarzenegger.com/en/actor/filmography/comma.asp.

17. Pauline Kael, "Thefts," *The New Yorker*, June 30, 1986, p. 51.

18. See Roger Ebert, Reviews, *Chicago Sun-Times*, June 12, 1987: http://rogerebert.suntimes.com/apps/pbcs.dll/article?AID=/19870612/REVIEWS/706120303/1023.

19. Vincent Canby, "U.S.-Soviet Buddy Movie With a Chicago Backdrop," *The New York Times*, June 17, 1988. Accessed July 26, 2006 (requires registration), http://movies2.nytimes.com/mem/movies/review.html?res=940DEEDA123AF934A25755C0A96E948260.

20. *Box Office*, 1988, R-77.

21. See http://www.schwarzenegger.com/en/actor/filmography/kinde.asp.

22. Robert Morris, "Recall: Not One for the Memory," *Village View*, June 1–7, 1990.

23. Terence Rafferty, "Terminated," *The New Yorker*, June 18, 1990, p. 51.

24. Maynard Good Stoddard, "Kindergarten Cop: A Classroom Caper," *The Saturday Evening Post*, January/February 1991, pp. 58–61.

25. *People*, January 21, 1991, pp. 118–119.

26. Michael Wilmington, "Kitschy, Kitschy Goo," *Los Angeles Times*, December 21, 1990, p. F1.

27. Ibid., p. F12.

28. Nancy Griffin, "How They Built the Bomb," *Premiere*, September 1993, p. 57.

29. Ibid., p. 112.

30. *Movieline*, May 1994, p. 40.

31. "Summer Movie Preview," *Entertainment Weekly*, May 27, 1994, p. 36.

32. Anne Thompson, "True Lies about James Cameron," *Entertainment Weekly*, July 29, 1994, p. 28.

33. David Hunter, "The Latest Action Hero," *LA Village View*, July 15–21, 1994, p. 17.

34. Elizabeth Pincus, "In Sickness and in Health," *LA Weekly*, July 22–28, 1994, p. 31.

35. Ibid.

36. Production Information: *Junior*, Universal Studios, p. 2.

37. Ibid., p. 3.

38. See http://www.schwarzenegger.com/en/actor/filmography/junio.asp.

39. Kenneth Turan, "Arnold's Mommy Syndrome," *Los Angeles Times*, November 23, 1994, p. F1.

40. See http://www.schwarzenegger.com/en/actor/filmography/erase.asp.

41. See http://blogs.salon.com/0002874/stories/2003/10/27/batmanAndRobin.html.

42. See http://www.fwfr.com/display.asp?id=341.

43. See http://www.nytimes.com/library/film/112499days-film-review.html.

44. See http://www.boxoffice.com/scripts/fiw.dll?GetReview&where=Name& terms=END+OF+DAY.

45. Elvis Mitchell, "'The Sixth Day': A Clone Ranger, Fighting the Future's Repetitive Fight," *The New York Times*, November 17, 2000. Accessed July 26, 2006 (requires registration), movies2.nytimes.com/mem/movies/review.html?res =940DE5D6153BF934A25752C1A9669C8B63.

46. Jeff O'Connell, "The 6th Day," *Muscle & Fitness* (January 2001): 88.

47. See http://www.schwarzenegger.com/en/actor/filmography/6thday.asp.

48. Elvis Mitchell, "Fed Up and Going After the Terrorist Himself," *The New York Times*, February 8, 2002. Accessed July 26, 2006, movies2.nytimes.com/ mem/movies/review.html?res=9804E3D9173CF93BA35751C0A9649C8B63.

49. Edward Guthmann, "'Damage' Beyond Repair: Schwarzenegger Can't Rescue Silly If Efficient Action Thriller," *San Francisco Chronicle*, February 8, 2002. p D1.

50. J. Hoberman, "Bully Pulpit," *The Village Voice*, February 8, 2002. Accessed July 26, 2006, http://www.villiagevoice.com/film/0207,hoberman,32232,20. html.

51. A.O. Scott, "A Monotonic Cyborg Learns to Say 'Pantsuit,'" *The New York Times*, July 1, 2003. Accessed July 26, 2006 (requires registration), http:// movies2.nytimes.com/mem/movies/review.html?res=9F01EFD6143AF932A357 54C0A9659C8B63.

52. Mike Clark, "Schwarzenegger Is Back, Barely, in 'Terminator 3,'" *USA Today*, July 7, 2003. Accessed, July 26, 2006, http://www.usatoday.com/life/ movies/reviews/2003-07-01-terminator_x.htm.

53. See Roger Ebert, Reviews, *Chicago Sun-Times*, June 16, 2004: http:// rogerebert.suntimes.com/apps/pbcs.dll/article?AID=/20040616/REVIEWS/ 406160301/1023.

Chapter 6

THE ARNOLD SCHWARZENEGGER OF ARNOLD SCHWARZENEGGERS

Long before the California recall election, indeed all through his body-building and film careers, Arnold Schwarzenegger had come to occupy a uniquely compelling place in the American imagination. Just as Americans had fused together the Terminator with the man who played him, we had also begun to blend together the larger-than-life Arnold Schwarzenegger and literally hundreds of ideas and things from everyday life. Arnold became a metaphor machine, generating comparisons between himself and numerous other objects, people, and processes in the culture.

A metaphor is a figure of speech, a way of putting words and ideas together that ends up being more than just a simple declarative statement. In metaphor, ideas associated with one category are applied to a completely different and seemingly unrelated category. So, for example, if we take a metaphor that has the structure "Ideas Are Food," from this metaphor we can generate phrases like, "The teacher *fed* us the answers to that question," or, "He told us his *half-baked* idea," or, "Her drawing was nothing but eye *candy*." Even Arnold's guiding principle of "staying hungry" fits this metaphoric mold.

Another aspect of metaphor has to do with creating a prototype, or ideal example, against which we can measure other things. For many years, people referring to something especially classy, expensive, and meticulously presented might say that it's the Rolls Royce of yachts, or restaurants, or investment. Arnold became one of these prototypes, the scale we used to measure the value of other things. As one journalist put it, "whenever someone succeeds … they're dubbed 'the Schwarzenegger' of their profession.[1] On the flipside, it's bad news for a product to lose its place on the Arnold-scale. As one car Web site tells us, the "Mustang isn't the Schwarzenegger of the muscle-car world nowadays."[2]

METAPHOR-MAN

It turns out that Arnold Schwarzenegger may be among the most powerful metaphor-machines the culture has ever seen. The man, his name, his movie roles (especially the Terminator), have become so deeply embedded in our everyday expressions, it is often difficult to avoid these metaphors. Arnold Schwarzenegger metaphors have become useful ways for us to describe things, measure them, evaluate them, and in general make sense of the world around us.

On the *Today Show* (July 17, 1995), the father of one of the hostages taken in Iraq during the first Gulf War commented that if he were Arnold Schwarzenegger, he would go in himself to rescue the hostages. What connection was that father making? He could have been acknowledging Arnold's physical strength, his movie characters' notoriety, his vast wealth and Hollywood power, his reputation for setting out on a mission and achieving it, or all of the above. Something about Arnold struck this man as being exactly the right metaphor to use in that very emotional moment.

The reference to Arnold in the previous example could be explained by the numerous movie characters he played and the rescue missions they completed. But what about the appearance of the Schwarzenegger metaphor in less likely places?[3] Take, for example, this use of both Arnold and the Terminator as a measure, of all things, of a tiny insect's power. The North Carolina Cooperative Extension Service, a government agency whose agriculture division gives advice on crops, pests, gardening, and raising animals, warns of a type of wasp that looks like "the Arnold Schwarzenegger of the ant world" and is invading area homes. The wasps are hard to get rid of permanently, they tell us: "In all likelihood, when next year rolls around *they'll be back*."[4]

Another example took place on a rural radio program that featured a discussion of a certain kind of sheep that has a genetic mutation. The odd mutation gives these sheep large, muscular buttocks and the ability to convert grass and grains into meat much more efficiently, almost at a whopping 50% increase in efficiency. Looking for a way to make this type of improvement in the animal understandable, a scientist explained, "If they were people, they would look like Arnold Schwarzenegger. They're big. And all muscle." They are the 'Schwarzenegger of sheep,' a print version of the same story explained.[5]

A new type of beef has recently become available on the market that has more muscle and less fat. According to one breeder of this special cattle, "It's the Arnold Schwarzenegger of cattle ... It's nutritionally correct meat with a high food value."[6] Keeping pace with the proliferation of such metaphors, a Web site about the giant Humboldt squid quotes a scientist who calls it the "Arnold of squids." [7] The animal metaphors are so widespread, and so strange, they can seem like they are just trying to be funny. But the fact that Arnold is a measure of quality and size in the animal world shows how much we rely on him for judging and measuring things, even when size is not important, but qualities like aggressiveness and persistence are.

A Web site for tourism in Florida describes a creature in state waters that it calls the "Arnold Schwarzenegger of the soft-shelled turtle world," a creature that "won't hesitate to defend its space" and has a sharp beak.[8] A discussion group for divers describes a dive off Palm Beach: "One coral hole was the home of the Arnold Schwarzenegger of crabs. This fellow was HUGE (his claws were as big as my hands), and he was not at all afraid of us. He kept pacing back and forth in his home, daring us to mess with him."[9] For the state of Georgia agricultural agents, a new bass appearing in their waters provides a fight for fishermen: "Anglers familiar with its fighting characteristics consider it the 'Arnold Schwarzenegger' of freshwater predator fish."[10]

Some of the Arnold metaphors are pretty far-fetched. A critic of Cardinal Joseph Ratzinger of the Roman Catholic Church, who went on to become Pope Benedict in 2005, called Ratzinger "the Schwarzenegger of doctrine" because of the strong hand he used in stating that the Catholic Church was the one, true church.[11] An article published in 2002 in a Miami arts and culture newspaper described how difficult it was to sample everything at a food and wine festival at Disney's Epcot, saying, "You'd have to be the Schwarzenegger of gastronomy to tackle it all in real time."[12] Less peculiar, but no less fascinating, is Marjorie Newlin, "the Arnold Schwarzenegger of grandmothers" in the National Enquirer in 1993 because, at age 72, she entered her newly developed muscular form into a bodybuilding competition.[13] Seventy-two-year-old grannies who go into bodybuilding demonstrate not only how plastic the human body is, but also that the model for fitness is one we've inherited from Arnold.

There is nothing natural about the connection between Arnold, a wasp, and the Terminator or between a sheep with large buttocks, a grandmother, and the greatest bodybuilder and the biggest movie star in the world. Yet somehow, these connections have come to be so thoroughly ingrained in everyday usage, they feel like perfectly ordinary ways to make sense of things in our world. This effect on our very language is remarkable evidence that shows how widespread and unique Arnold Schwarzenegger's influence really is.

AN ARNOLD METAPHOR FOR EVERY OCCASION

What other figure in American culture, real or cinematic, could cover as many subjects as Arnold Schwarzenegger does? The list of Arnold and terminator metaphors is so long, it would take another book or two to list them all! But a few more examples can show the range these metaphors and cultural references cover:

Arnold as a measure of power:
- A radio announcer says of Russian leader Boris Yeltsin, "Y'know, he's not exactly the Arnold Schwarzenegger of world leaders."

Arnold as a reference for excellence or achievement:
- In a report looking at the history of the stock market, one of the market ratings services is described as having new confidence to judge the value of stocks. The service in this otherwise sober market is said to ride about "like the Arnold Schwarzenegger of balance sheets."[14]

Arnold as a model of morphing or metamorphosis:
- In a 1991 *Los Angeles Times* editorial about David Duke, former Klansmen turned politician: "David Duke transforms himself from klan wizard to racial moderate and champion of the dispossessed as easily as Arnold Schwarzenegger's evil 'Terminator' metamorphoses into a noble android in 'Terminator II.'"[15]

Arnold as a measure of individual persistence and determination:
- In a 1991 *Los Angeles Times* article on police chief Daryl Gates: "Even Arnold Schwarzenegger pales in comparison to Gates' cybernetic tenacity."[16]

Arnold as the standard of great strength:
- 1992 *Los Angeles Times* article on the Landers earthquake described on man's home as looking like "it had been trashed in a 'Terminator' movie."[17]
- A text on the history of ancient theater says that Herakles [Hercules] was "the Arnold Schwarzenegger of his day."[18]

Arnold as an indicator of poor speech and acting styles:
- 1998 review of the film *Firestorm:* "Long has the steroid-buffed look of an action hero. But his expressionless face and monotone delivery make even Arnold Schwarzenegger at his most robotic seem like a hypersensitive crybaby."[19]

Arnold as a sign of his own influence:
- A 1990 *Newsweek* article on male pectoral implants states, "... maybe it's a sign of the Schwarzeneggerization of society."[20] In 2004 the comparison is still being made by a plastic surgeon who does biceps implants: "It takes an hour and once it's performed, you've got the biceps of Schwarzenegger."[21]

There are Schwarzenegger's of wine and beer and Terminator stout and mustard. The Schwarzenegger of wines is so strong, it has "a grrr wine that grabs your tongue and shakes it around."[22] There are Schwarzenegger's of climbing, skateboarding, pediatricians, pornography, pianists, dinosaurs, oxen, goats, cattle, birds, trees, invasive plants, dogs and cats, turtles, crabs, trash companies, Velcro fasteners, iPod cases, cars, motorcycles, and Supreme Court justices.

Perhaps the most publicized connection between Arnold Schwarzenegger and an idea or product has been the association of both Arnold and the Terminator with the all-terrain vehicle, The Hummer. Arnold was the very first American civilian to obtain the military vehicle, the High Mobility Multi-purpose Wheeled Vehicle—or HumVee—that was popularized during Operation Desert Storm in the 1991 Gulf War. Since then, Arnold has been called both the official and the unofficial ambassador for the Hummer, and the vehicle has been compared to Arnold himself in a series of attractive ad campaigns. Once the HumVee was changed into the Hummer (which is what Arnold apparently called this unique vehicle), and Arnold convinced General Motors to make the Hummer available to the general public, the cyborg connection between the car and the man who gave it its new stylish name was forever fused. The advertisement for the first retail model of the Hummer tells the tale:

> Think of it as Arnold on Wheels.
> Almost nothing on the face of the earth is tougher than Arnold.
> Almost nothing. Meet HUMMER for 1994. Tougher, stronger, more powerful than ever. Like Arnold, it can go places the others wouldn't dare to go. Or maybe even want to. It can

do things the others wouldn't think of doing. It will take you there. And, like Arnold, it will be back.

HUMMER: Nothing is tougher. Hasta la vista, baby.[23]

As if this connection between man and machine were not already as strong as it could be, announcements for the 2001 luxury edition of the Hummer dissolved any distinction between the two. One article in the *Los Angeles Times* called the new Hummers "Sport-Brutes: Like Schwarzenegger with Bumpers."[24] A promotion for another new Hummer—the H2—on *Good Morning America* featured Arnold popping out of one of these "brawny four-wheel drive boulder crawlers with military roots" and proclaiming that the Hummer is a truck with hair on its chest.

Motor Trend's review of the 2003 H2 describes it as having "Schwarzenegger muscle to go with its Schwarzenegger looks."[25] Marty Padgett, author of the book *Hummer*, writes, "Hop in the driver's seat and you can become Arnold Schwarzenegger's Terminator."[26] Nowadays, that last statement is especially ambiguous, and maybe more than a little ironic. The "ethical values" that define Hummer include an almost complete disregard for fuel-efficiency and an insistence on occupying a disproportionately large piece of the road. Perhaps Padgett said it most poetically when he wrote: "HUMMERs are lethal weapons—and toys. They're obnoxiously large vehicles that … do things few other vehicles on the face of the earth can do. They can launch TOW missiles with stunning accuracy, clabber down stone steps like mountain goats, and draw a crowd of teenagers more quickly than a vacant Xbox or Britney Spears."[27] In other words, a HUMMER is really a heck of a lot like Arnold Schwarzenegger … and vice versa.

To be the measure of so many important things—right and wrong, good and bad, real and unreal, proper or improper, big and small, valuable or worthless—is an amazing feat. It's easy to comprehend how a constantly widening context for Arnold references would keep Schwarzenegger foregrounded in the American imagination. In a sense, all these metaphors give Arnold a podium from which to speak. On the radio, in television, on Web sites, at congressional hearings, in magazines and newspapers, in children's videos and cartoons, at public lectures, or in courtrooms, Arnold can have his say without having to make a direct appearance. It is amazing that he helps define what can be seen as valuable, what can be thought to be powerful, and what can be accepted as important; he doesn't even have to show up to enforce his vision of this world: We do it for him. Whether it is through an obscure reference like that of the "Schwarzenegger of sheep" or the most familiar ones to the Terminator, these are impressive uses of Arnold to define our world. There have been a number of Schwarzeneggers in the world, and Arnold and Maria have produced four more Schwarzenegger offspring, but Arnold is the Schwarzenegger of Schwarzeneggers—virtually immeasurable in scale.

NOTES

1. Mehammed Mack, "Ungh-nold!" *The Daily Californian*, Retrieved 9/8/2003 from http://www.dailycal.org/article.php?id=12611.

2. See http://www.smartmoney.com/autos/newcars/index.cfm?story = april2005.

3. This and many of the following references are on the web, but because web links can change so often, the best way to find these examples and more is to Google "the Schwarzenegger of" with the quotes.

4. See http://ipm.ncsu.edu/current_ipm/03PestNews/03News17/resident.html.

5. See http://www.geneimprint.com/articles/?y=Press&q=callipyge/ABCruralnews/abcruralnews.html.

6. See http://www.montanarange.com/news_montana_range.html.

7. See http://www.prometheus6.org/node/3101.

8. See http://fortmyers-sanibel.com/everything_to_do/nature/softshellturtle.php.

9. See http://www.diveatlas.com/travel/florida5.asp.

10. See http://county.ces.uga.edu/habersham/spm/spring.html.

11. See http://www.shipoffools.com/Cargo/Features00/Features/Dominus200.html.

12. See http://www.miaminewtimes.com/issues/2002–12–05/dish.html.

13. Bill O'Neill, "72-year-old Granny Is a Champion Bodybuilder," *National Enquirer*, August 10, 1993, p. 33.

14. "4th Quarter Review 2001: Market Overview," Miller/Howard Investment, Inc., 2001, p 3. Accessed July 26, 2006, http://mhinverst.com/qtr/4qtr/01.pdf.

15. Bruce Shulman, "Dark Side of American Dream: When Reinventing Past Means Forgetting It," *Los Angeles Times*, November 3, 1991, p. M2.

16. Al Martinez, "Life Goes On," *Los Angeles Times*, July 11, 1991, p. 2B.

17. Sheryl Stolberg, "In Lander, Temblors Are Talk of the Town," *Los Angeles Times*, June 29, 1992, p.A7.

18. See http://emc.elte.hu/~pinter/szoveg/theatre.pdf.

19. Stephen Holden, "A Ravenous Forest Fire Doused by Testosterone," *New York Times*, January 9, 1998.

20. E. Yoffe, "Valley of the Silicone Dolls," *Newsweek*, November 26, 1990, p. 72.

21. See http://www.msnbc.msn.com/id/5006801/.

22. See http://msnbc.msn.com/id/7000183/site/newsweek/.

23. The ad appeared nationwide, including in *Hemispheres*, United Airline's in-flight magazine, June 1994, p. 60.

24. Terril Yue Jones, *Los Angeles Times*, May 2, 2001, G1.

25. See http://www.motortrend.com/features/performance/112_0308_2003_lingenfelter_hummer_h2/index.html.

26. Martin Padgett, *Hummer: How a Little Truck Company Hit the Big Time, Thanks to Saddam, Schwarzenegger and* GM (St. Paul, MN: MBI Publishing, 2004), p 174.

27. Ibid., p 244.

As a teen, Arnold picked up his first bar bell and decided that he wanted to be a great bodybuilder. By the 1970's, he was considered the best built man in the world. Courtesy of Photofest.

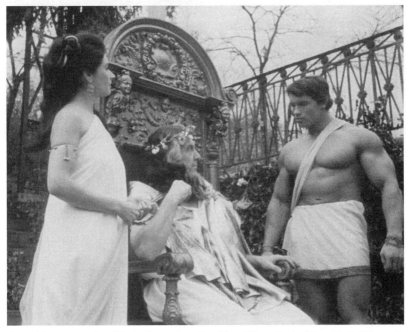

Arnold appeared as Hercules in his first film, *Hercules in New York*. Though widely criticized by critics and movie fans, this film opened doors for its star. Courtesy of Photofest.

Arnold became an American citizen in 1983. Courtesy of Photofest.

Part of Arnold's "Master Plan" included working in the movies as an actor. Playing the character Conan launched his career into stardom. Arnold is pictured here in *Conan the Destroyer*, which was released in 1984. Courtesy of Photofest.

In the film *Terminator 2: Judgment Day*, Arnold's character has changed from assassin to protector and from evil to heroic. Courtesy of Photofest.

In the 1994 film *True Lies*, Arnold portrayed Harry Tasker, a man leading a double life as both a sophisticated spy and a nerdy computer salesman. Courtesy of Photofest.

During his campaign for California governor, Arnold was accused of "grop-ing," or inappropriately touching women. Arnold's campaign had women at his rallies wear T-shirts and carry signs that said, "Remarkable Women Join Arnold." Photo courtesy of Louise Krasniewicz.

Arnold appears at his last public rally before the October 2003 election. He is sworn in as Governor of California in November. Photo courtesy of Louise Krasniewicz.

Arnold is pictured here with his wife, Maria Shriver at the Cannes Film Festival in 2003. The couple, who first met in 1977 at a charity tennis match, married in 1986. Maria, who is famous in her own right, has been a journalist, news anchor, successful author, and is the mother of four children. Courtesy of Photofest.

Chapter 7

CITIZEN ARNOLD

On September 16, 1983, Arnold Schwarzenegger became a citizen of the United States. Twenty-one years later, in a speech to more than 200 newly naturalized sailors and U.S. Marines from 43 different countries, California Governor Arnold Schwarzenegger said: "This country was always known as the land of opportunity, the greatest country in the world ... I was very fortunate because this country opened up its arms to me, and gave me the opportunities to reach my goals and much more."[1] For Arnold, becoming an American citizen was one of the big milestones of his life. Why? For one thing, it was the culmination of the kind of large-scale dream for which he was already famous. For another, it was, for Arnold, confirmation of his desire to become an integral part of the American cultural landscape. It's one thing to be a famous foreigner living in the United States; it's quite another to be able to tell the world, "I am an American." As Arnold himself put it, "As long as I live, I will never forget that day 21 years ago when I raised my hand and took the oath of citizenship. Do you know how proud I was? I was so proud that I walked around with an American flag around my shoulders all day long."[2]

BECOMING NATURALIZED

What does it take to become an American citizen? There a number of general requirements:

- A period of continuous residence and physical presence in the United States;
- Residence in a particular United States Citizenship and Immigration Services (USCIS) District prior to filing;

- An ability to read, write, and speak English;
- A knowledge and understanding of U.S. history and government;
- Good moral character;
- Attachment to the principles of the U.S. Constitution; and,
- Favorable disposition toward the United States.[3]

It's safe to say that by 1983, Arnold met all of these requirements fairly easily. He had been living in the United States for 15 years. While his accent was still pronounced, he was fluent in English and had mastered many of the language's peculiar idioms. He had a reasonable knowledge of American history and a deep interest in the history of American politics. Arnold's interest in, and commitment to, American principles of governance and law had been evident from his decision, in 1968, to be a Republican like President Richard Nixon. As for his "favorable disposition toward the United States," few in America could be described as more in love with the country, its people, and its culture.

The feeling seemed to be mutual. Indeed, few people have ever been so completely and powerfully embraced by a culture than Arnold, and he appreciated the fact that America had rolled out the red-carpeted welcome mat for him. "I was born in Europe … and I've traveled all over the world. I can tell you that there is no place, no country, that is more compassionate, more generous, more accepting, and more welcoming than the United States of America."[4]

Any possible questions about Arnold's "moral character" were neutralized by his relationship with Maria Shriver. Shriver is the daughter of Eunice Kennedy Shriver and Sergeant Shriver and the niece of the assassinated U.S. President John F. Kennedy. Arnold and Maria met in 1977 at a charity tennis match. Arnold and Maria married in 1986. Arnold, the staunch Republican, married into the most famous and powerful Democratic family in the nation.

Maria Shriver Schwarzenegger had a career as a news anchor and journalist before her marriage, and she kept up aspects of that career until Arnold became governor. She and Arnold have four children, the oldest born in 1989 and the youngest in 1997. Considered glamorous and famous in her own right, Maria is not only an author, entrepreneur, and philanthropist, but she is, as she states on her Web site, "mother, wife, daughter, sister, and friend."[5] Like her father, who started the Peace Corps, she promotes volunteer work and acts as Honorary Chair of California's Service Corps, an organization that encourages citizens to engage in acts of service to improve the life of all Californians.

Becoming a citizen would mean far more to Arnold than the formality of naturalization. To him, it meant the beginning of an unprecedented flurry of activity not only in service to his career, but in service to his newly adoptive homeland—America, and especially California. Over the next few years, America would witness a staggering display of Arnold's power: in the box office, in the commercial bodybuilding world, in humanitarian causes, and within just 7 years of his becoming a naturalized citizen of the United States, in American politics. At every turn, Arnold attributed his achievements to the opportunities afforded him by the United States. "Everything I have—my career, my success, my family—I owe to America."[6]

FIRST YEAR AS CITIZEN ARNOLD

Some newly naturalized U.S. citizens take the opportunity to go after that job they've always wanted, or to make an investment, or simply to cast their first vote in a general election. But it's a very rare brand-new citizen who has a year like Arnold's!

Within a year of becoming a U.S. citizen, Arnold Released *Conan the Destroyer*, out-earned every other movie in 1984, grossing more than $100 million dollars worldwide. Nineteen eighty-four also saw the blockbuster release of *The Terminator*, and, wasting no time, Arnold was at work on another epic battle film, *Red Sonja*. That year, the National Association of Theater Owners (NATO) voted Arnold "International Star of the Year." Always eager to do enormous amounts of work, Arnold's new status as an American seemed to propel him to a new intensity. Being a fully recognized American also provided Arnold with just the right motivation, in 1985, to propose marriage to Maria Shriver. The two took their vows in 1986, "securing his ties to the United States forever."[7] Movies, awards, and marriage—for starters!

HUSBAND ARNOLD

Lifetime TV called it one of the "weddings of a lifetime": "The excitement about the star-studded wedding of Maria Shriver to movie superstar Arnold Schwarzenegger energized all of Cape Cod in the summer of 1986."[8] Nearly 400 guests attended the lavish event on April 26, hosted by Maria's famous parents, Eunice and Sergeant Shriver, at the Kennedy "compound" in Hyannis, Massachusetts. Beneath her elegant gown, Maria wore sneakers—not because she was marrying the bodybuilding and athletic star, but because she had a pair of broken toes! According to the

Lifetime TV Web site, the night before the wedding, Arnold's mother, Aurelia, hosted a party that "celebrated the couple's different backgrounds with an 'Austrian clambake' that included lobster and Wiener schnitzel."[9]

The marriage of Arnold and Maria represented for many the creation of a true "power couple," each with a legitimate claim to widespread influence and wealth. The two had met in 1977 when Maria's brother Bobby invited Arnold to the annual Robert F. Kennedy Pro Celebrity Tennis Tournament in Forrest Hills, New York. Arnold had already achieved national recognition for his appearance in the 1977 bodybuilding film, *Pumping Iron*, and Bobby Shriver thought Arnold would be a real crowd-pleaser. Teamed up with former football great, Rosie Greer, Arnold and his partner were getting clobbered in doubles by a pair of kids. So, to make things more interesting, the big-bellied Rosie and the giant-muscled Arnold took their shirts off and played to the delighted crowd. That afternoon, Maria invited her new acquaintance, Arnold, back to the family compound in Hyannis Port. Maria said, "I was pretty sure when I met him that I would marry him … I admired his independence, his focus, his drive, his humor. I thought I would have a challenging life with him. Not an easy life, but an interesting one."[10]

In keeping with his lifelong theme of growing larger and more important, Arnold had, by 1985, established a string of successes that would have been lifetime achievements for most people. He had half a dozen hit movies, dozens of bodybuilding titles, the very public engagement to a charismatic member of the Kennedy clan, large real estate holdings, national and international notoriety, wealth beyond most people's imagination, and many more years of mega-stardom ahead of him. In a national poll conducted by *Muscle & Fitness* magazine in 1987, Arnold was voted best bodybuilder of all time. As a U.S. citizen, Arnold was achieving the kind of greatness he had not only dreamed about, but he had always planned. It was time to start the engines of another vehicle—one he'd long anticipated: politics.

Some might argue that Arnold's determination to enter American political life began with his arrival in the United States. But Arnold is more systematic than that. It's fine to aspire to political power, but one has to put more than just one's money where one's mouth is. Arnold knew that American political power was an important piece of the project—what we might call *the Arnold project*—and to acquire that power, citizen Arnold was going to have to use the kind of clever strategy for which he was already famous. To the uninitiated, Arnold's first true American political achievement might seem almost accidental.

But to Arnold-watchers, 1990 saw Arnold once again in the right place at the right time.

PRESIDENTIAL APPOINTMENT

Remember now, in 1968 when Arnold was just a new arrival in the United States, he'd seen a television program on which President Richard Nixon was speaking. Arnold's roommate translated Nixon's speech into German for Arnold, and upon hearing Nixon's message, Arnold decided that he, too, was a Republican. In a sense, Nixon became Arnold Schwarzenegger's political muse.

Digging just a bit further back into history, in 1956, under President Eisenhower, Vice President Richard Nixon was appointed Chair—of all things—of the newly created President's Council on Youth Fitness. This was a cabinet-level appointment, and the Executive Order featured a single objective: to raise public awareness about the need for youth fitness. In 1957, The President's Council sponsored the first Conference on Physical Fitness of Youth, held at the U.S. Military Academy in West Point, New York. At that conference, participants developed a plan to examine the physical fitness levels of school children across the country. This study of 8,500 boys and girls led to a national program whereby children between the ages of 5 and 12 would be tested annually on their physical fitness. Today, this program is called the President's Challenge.[11]

In 1961, President John F. Kennedy changed the name of the council to the President's Council on Physical Fitness. The Council would now concern itself not only with younger children, but with all children and, as a new feature, with adults as well. Kennedy added a second objective to the original Executive Order, in which he called upon all citizens, civic groups, and youth organizations to participate in promoting fitness. Around the country, in magazines, on television, billboards, and elsewhere, a nationwide public service advertising campaign kept physical fitness in the forefront of people's attention. President Kennedy himself showed his support of this new consciousness by going on some of the 50-mile hikes. Elementary and secondary schools with outstanding records of promoting physical education were showcased at special centers established to further promote fitness in youth.

A couple of years later, President Lyndon Johnson, who had assumed office after President Kennedy's assassination in 1963, changed the council's name once again to the President's Council on Physical Fitness and Sports. From 1964 to 1967, the new Council was chaired by baseball great, Stan Musial. This new version of the Council was charged, by the president "to encourage lasting fitness gains through sports and games."[12] Johnson added new objectives to the Executive Order. In 1965, the second national fitness survey was conducted, this time of children between the ages of 10 and 17. The following year, President Johnson commissioned the *Presidential Physical Fitness Award* to be granted to boys and girls for outstanding fitness and sports achievements.

President Nixon, in 1969, maintained the nation's focus on fitness and sports by appointing popular astronaut James Lovell to the position of Chair of the Council, and by instituting, in 1972, the *Presidential Sports Award* to further promote fitness and sports among children of all ages. Both Presidents Ford and Carter followed suit during their terms, continuing the president's active support for the Council on Physical Fitness and Sports. During Ronald Reagan's tenure as president, the Council saw a surge of new initiatives under Council Chair George Allen. Coach Allen's goals included the creation of national fitness foundations, a fitness academy, fitness forums, and an award called "The Healthy American Fitness Leaders Award;" and under Allen's leadership, the U.S. Postal Service issued a physical fitness postage stamp. In 1984, the same year that Arnold Schwarzenegger became the "Terminator," President Reagan established the first National Women's Leadership Conference on Fitness. First Lady Nancy Reagan served as Honorary Chair.

But it was George H. Bush in 1990 who did something that put the President's Council on Physical Fitness and Sports into the brightest limelight: He appointed Arnold Schwarzenegger Chair. Things had come full circle for Arnold! He now occupied the position once held by his first American political hero, Richard Nixon.

Arnold would almost single-handedly transform the Council into a living example of his ability to capitalize on opportunity. Arnold promptly instituted the "Great American Workouts" that were held on the White House lawn. Whereas previous Council Chairs had conducted the business of national physical fitness in fairly limited fashion, Arnold took it upon himself to visit all 50 states, where he promoted fitness, health, sports, and nutrition. In effect, he was on the road not only to spread a message about fitness, but, more significantly about a very special man: himself!

Committed to restoring physical fitness programs to schools across the country, Arnold tapped into America's competitive spirit within his first few days as Chair: "If you compare the physical fitness standards in this country with other countries, America is falling behind. It's important we get back those physical education classes and let the youth know it is important to exercise … You aren't likely to feel fantastic until you accept exercise as a way of life."[13] Arnold "declared war on 'Couch Potatoes'" and other unfit, overweight, inactive children and adults. Such lack of concern for physical education and health was, in Arnold's view, "America's secret tragedy."[14]

Fitness on a national scale was not new for Arnold, however. Since 1979, Arnold has served as the International Weight Training Coach of Special Olympics. The Special Olympics had a dramatic start on July 20th, 1968. Eunice Kennedy Shriver—Arnold's future mother-in-law—organized the First International Special Olympics Games at Chicago's Soldier Field. Years earlier, Mrs. Shriver had established a camp for the mentally retarded. "She saw that people with mental retardation were far more capable in sports and physical activities than many experts thought."[15] In the nearly 40 years since the creation of the Special Olympics, millions of people have participated. There is a Special Olympics chapter in every state in America along with a number of American territories and around 150 countries throughout the world. In 2004, President George W. Bush signed into law H.R. 5131, the "Special Olympics Sport and Empowerment Act of 2004," guaranteeing support for the Special Olympics. This, too, was a way for Arnold's efforts to come full circle. Twenty-five years earlier, when Arnold first put his muscles into the Special Olympics arena, who could have imagined that a *second* President Bush would, once again, reaffirm Arnold's efforts?

If these activities—body-building greatness, movie stardom, presidential appointment, famous marriage, high-profile weight trainer in Special Olympics, real estate owner (Arnold purchased a number of commercial real estate holdings in Southern California and co-owns a one million square-foot urban entertainment and retail shopping center located in the northeast quadrant of Columbus, Ohio, which was opened in 1999),[16] and more—were "all" Arnold had managed in his career, everyone would say that he'd done an unbelievable amount of truly remarkable things in his lifetime. During this time, in 1979, Arnold also found the time to graduate from the University of Wisconsin Superior with a B.A. in business and international economics. And he had done all these things in just about 25 years in the united states. Arnold was not, however, about to rest on this record of accomplishments. Always a champion of fitness for both children and adults, Citizen Arnold would turn his considerable organizational talents to yet another aspect of society that would demonstrate, yet again, his effusively "favorable disposition toward the United States": the after-school activities of children.

In 1991, during his term as Chair of the President's Council on Physical Fitness and Sports, Schwarzenegger involved himself in yet another effort to provide guidance and training to America's youth. This time, it was the Los Angeles Inner City Games that drew his attention. This was a kind of "mini-Olympics designed to help kids say 'no' to drugs and violence and 'yes' to fitness as a way of life."[17] Not content to participate on the sidelines, Arnold helped establish the Inner City Games Foundation in 1995 and has served as its Chair. A little over 10 years later, this program is nationally recognized and its new name is After-School All-Stars.

Of course, it's not always so easy for Arnold to put his vision into practice. In 2002, Arnold sponsored and won passage of an after-school initiative labeled Proposition 49. He spent more than a million dollars of his own money and solicited donations from many of his colleagues in Hollywood to help support the bill. "There are millions of children floating around after school with no place to go and no adult supervision," Arnold told a group of potential contributors.[18] However, not everyone agreed that this bill should be funded. It would mean the state of California would have to dedicate $550 million per year to the after-school programs, and many felt that the bill was too expensive. Some did not like the fact that the proposal had come from a Hollywood celebrity who might be sharpening up his political skills for a run for state office. By August of 2005, Proposition 49 was approved yet still un-enforced. But in January of 2006, Proposition 49, more specifically called the After School Education and Safety Act, was revisited by the new Governor of California, who just happened to be … Arnold Schwarzenegger! As you might imagine, this time around, the initiative received the necessary funding.

CLASSIC ARNOLD

Just 6 years after becoming a U.S. citizen, Arnold Schwarzenegger, along with one of his business associates, James Lorimer, created an event that would bring together the country's top bodybuilders and other athletes and, more significantly, memorialize one of America's most ardent citizens: Arnold himself! The event was called "The Arnold Classic" and was launched in 1989. Schwarzenegger and Lorimer had collaborated previously to promote the Mr. Olympia contest in 1976, and they created the Ms. Olympia contest in 1986 in Columbus, Ohio, the very same city they chose for what is now "the largest fitness weekend in the world."[19]

By 1993, the Arnold Classic was just one big part of the Arnold Fitness Expo, an annual event where hundreds of vendors converge to display the latest in fitness wear, fitness gear, workout equipment, and more. According to Arnold's Web site, the Expo alone draws more than 40,000 people annually.[20]

Over the years, the Expo and the Arnold Classic have grown and are, themselves, now part of an even larger annual celebration called the Arnold Fitness Weekend. For two days every March, athletes participate and compete in a variety of events, including the Ms. International competition (women's bodybuilding), the Arnold Martial Arts Festival (demonstration and competition), Fitness International (women's overall fitness), and, what is for many the highlight of the weekend, the Arnold Fitness Training Seminar conducted by none other than Citizen Arnold himself.

While there have been athletes who have had tournaments created in their names, none have ever managed to produce so enormous a sports and fitness event that has become part of Americana. Few have ever made so much of their hard-earned status as a U.S. citizen. Leave it to Arnold, then, to continue to scramble the American imagination by transforming the way people think about party politics. Citizen Arnold, with his political affiliation with the Republican Party, along with his very public marriage to staunch Democrat Maria, was now going to force his fans and followers—and his detractors—to rethink the whole distinction between Democrat and Republican.

NOTES

1. "Schwarzenegger speaks to newest citizens," *Navy Newstand: the source for Navy news*, February 11, 2004Accessed July 26, 2006, http://www.navy.mil/search/display.asp?story_id=11731.

2. See 2004 Republican National Convention Address, August 31, 2004: http://www.brainyquote.com/quotes/quotes/a/arnoldschw168330.html.

3. United States Citizenship and Immigration Services Web site: http://uscis.gov/graphics/services/natz/index.htm.

4. See 2004 Republican National Convention Address.

5. Maria Shriver's Web site: http://www.firstlady.ca.gov/state/firstlady/fl_homepage.jsp.

6. See 2004 Republican National Convention Address.

7. See Jennifer and Peter Wipf, "Arnold Schwarzenegger—an American Dream" on Arnold Schwarzenegger—an Austrian Immigrant Web site. Accessed July 26, 2006, http://immigration.about.com/od/infilmtvandtheater/a/Arnold-schwarz.htm.

8. See http://www.lifetimetv.com/shows/weddings/kennedy/maria.html.

9. Ibid.

10. See http://www.rom101.com/storyview.jsp?storyid=465.

11. See the President's Council on Physical Fitness and Sports Web site: http://www.fitness.gov/about_history.htm.

12. Ibid.

13. See "Red, white, and blue fitness—President's council on Physical Fitness and Sports," *American Fitness*, May/June 1990. Available: http://www.findarticles. com/p/articles/mi_m0675/is_n3_v8/ai_8477706.

14. Arnold Schwarzenegger, "A Message to You," Available: http://www. schwarzenegger.com/en/athlete/message/index.asp?sec=athlete&subsec=message.

15. See Special Olympics on Schwarzenegger.com Web site: http://www. schwarzenegger.com/en/activist/specialolympics/activist_specialolympics_eng_legacy_435.asp?sec=activist&subsec=specialolympics.

16. See "Arnold Schwarzenegger" at http://www.filmbug.com/db/1083.

17. See "Arnold Schwarzenegger Biography." *German American History and Heritage*. Accessed July 26, 2006, http://www.germanheritage.com/biographies/ mtoz/schwarzenegger.html

18. Alexa H. Bluth, "Schwarzenegger leads battle for after school measure," at SFGate.com, October 19, 2002: http://www.sfgate.com/cgi-bin/article.cgi?file=/ news/archive/2002/10/19/state1305EDT0039.DTL.

19. See http://www.arnoldexpo.com/2006_strength_summit.asp.

20. See http://www.schwarzenegger.com/en/athlete/arnoldclassic/index.asp?sec =athlete&subsec=arnoldclassic.

Chapter 8

REPUBLICAN ARNOLD

Nothing introduces the snooze factor more quickly into a book like this than talking about traditional Republican and Democratic politics … ZZZZZZZzzzzzzzzz. Politics in this country, which could be a fascinating exercise in history, economics, and culture, tends instead to be a painful exercise in influence peddling, partisan decision-making, and character assassination.

But imagine that you are Arnold Schwarzenegger. You have been elected as the governor of the state of California, your adopted home. You have seen both your American Dream and your Master Plan fulfilled, and you have always been passionate about teaching your ideas to others. Whether it has been showing others how to build their bodies, convincing politicians to support fitness and afterschool programs, or giving moviegoers a good story to watch, your work requires an audience that can share your enthusiasm for an idea or a goal or a plan. Now you have been invited to address the national convention of your political party, the most important political gathering of the year. You may have just ventured way beyond your original dreams, and you are about to take full advantage of it.

THE REPUBLICAN NATIONAL CONVENTION 2004

Every four years, in preparation for the presidential elections that take place in November, the two major American political parties (the Democrats and the Republicans) hold large meetings called conventions. At these political nominating conventions, the delegates agree upon a candidate to represent their party in the upcoming election. The conventions also determine the party's platform of ideas and goals which will guide their agenda in the following years.

These major political conventions have become more like pep rallies in recent years, with the real political work of the parties being done elsewhere. But they are important ceremonial occasions, and they include many speeches in the days leading up to the actual introduction of the candidate. The speeches are often an opportunity for the party to promote up-and-coming party members or to highlight its best known supporters. Enter Arnold Schwarzenegger.

What were the Republicans thinking when they had Arnold Schwarzenegger stand up at their 2004 national convention to give a speech about what it means to be a Republican? Sure the guy is charismatic and introduces the Hollywood "bling" factor into a New York arena full of Iowa farmers and Ohio suburbanites. But the criticism that he is a Republican in Democratic clothing, a traitor to the conservative agenda, or a Republican only when it suits him did not seem to matter to Arnold or the Republican National Committee.

It would be interesting to know what kind of negotiations had to go on behind the scenes to get Arnold to stand up and identify so strongly with the political party that opposes much of his social agenda. It hardly seems likely that Schwarzenegger really is a die-hard Republican, a party loyalist who is actually "the Disney version" of Vice President Dick Cheney.[1] The two men are not only at opposite ends of the fitness coin, but they are not even often on the same side of the political divide. There is just too big a gap between the two on policies and opinions for the comparison to be worthwhile. Republican party celebrants were certainly not there to be instructed by Conan the Republican in the fine art of being a party member. Arnold has contributed service and money to the Republican party and ran as a Republican in the recall election, but he has never towed the party line.

Yet Arnold's speech, a combination of how he fulfilled the American Dream and why being a Republican made him do it, was widely applauded and has been endlessly cited by outsiders as the best thing about the convention. The text of the speech has spread like a virus across the Internet and is now available at dozens of sites.[2]

WHAT IS A REPUBLICAN?

At the Republican National Convention in 2004, the incumbent president George W. Bush was already the selected candidate of the party, so there was no mystery or anticipation that could be used to build interest in the nominating process. But one of the highlights of the convention for national television audiences was the appearance of the recently elected governor of California. Arnold appeared in prime time on television, and his appearance was designed to draw an audience to the event that night, which also featured the President's young twin daughters, who started their speech by declaring that Arnold was "awesome."

Arnold's opening lines showed more humor and self-confidence than all of the other speeches combined (except, perhaps, the goofy presentations by President Bush's troublesome twins daughters, Jenna and Barbara):

> Thank you.
> What a greeting!
> This is like winning an Oscar! ...
> As if I would know! Speaking of acting, one of my movies was called True Lies. It's what the Democrats should have called their convention.

Besides showing tremendous stage presence and humor, Arnold presented himself as better than the Democrats, as the best model of an American, an immigrant, and a politician. Whatever the organizers of this prime-time television presentation had in mind, what they got was Arnold's blueprint for remaking the Republican Party in his own image, without apologies and with no prisoners taken, a real terminator of politics as usual. Arnold's version of Republicanism and the American Dream tugged at the heart-strings, was all-inclusive, and even had Democrat Maria Shriver smiling.

Arnold often tells the story of how he became a Republican. He repeated it again that night:

> I finally arrived here in 1968. I had empty pockets, but I was full of dreams. The presidential campaign was in full swing. I remember watching the Nixon and Humphrey presidential race on TV. A friend who spoke German and English translated for me. I heard Humphrey saying things that sounded like socialism, which is what I had just left. But then I heard Nixon speak. He was talking about free enterprise, getting government off your back, lowering taxes and strengthening the military. Listening to Nixon speak sounded more like a breath of fresh air.
>
> I said to my friend, "What party is he?" My friend said, "He's a Republican." I said, "Then I am a Republican!" And I've been a Republican ever since! And trust me, in my wife's family, that's no small achievement!

The traditional differences between the Republicans and the Democrats is that the Republicans favor a small federal government, believing individual citizens are better at making their own decisions and guiding their own lives. This means a belief in lowering taxes and a pro-business stance, as well as a general opposition to regulations on business practices. This has not kept the Republicans from being socially conservative and trying to regulate marriage, oppose abortion, and eliminate the separation of church and state. Democrats, on the other hand, favor having the government take an active role in helping support citizens who don't have the necessary resources. Their social agenda calls for regulation on industry that does not control itself well enough and government protection of the right of individuals to make decisions that center on privacy.

Schwarzenegger's stands on many significant issues are in direct contrast to those positions officially taken by the Republican party. Yet it was Arnold's job in his speech to define what it meant to be a Republican. His speech addressed this seeming contradiction:

> Now, many of you out there tonight are "Republican" like me in your hearts and in your beliefs ... And maybe just maybe you don't agree with this party on every single issue. I say to you tonight I believe that's not only okay, that's what's great about this country. Here we can respectfully disagree and still be patriotic, still be American, and still be good Republicans.

The next list of qualifications for being a Republican was so cleverly written that even die-hard Democrats and independents could see themselves in all or parts of it:

> If you believe that government should be accountable to the people, not the people to the government ... then you are a Republican! If you believe a person should be treated as an individual, not as a member of an interest group ... then you are a Republican! If you believe your family knows how to spend your money better than the government does ... then you are a Republican! If you believe our educational system should be held accountable for the progress of our children ... then you are a Republican! If you believe this country, not the United Nations, is the best hope of democracy in the world ... then you are a Republican! And, ladies and gentlemen ... if you believe we must be fierce and relentless and terminate terrorism ... then you are a Republican.

The final criteria not only set the Republicans apart from the rest, but separated the men from the "girlie men" just as Arnold had done in California:

> There is another way you can tell you're a Republican. You have faith in free enterprise, faith in the resourcefulness of the American people ... and faith in the U.S. economy. To those critics who are so pessimistic about our economy, I say: "Don't be economic girlie men!"

THE OFFICIAL REPUBLICANS

The official Republican platform on almost all social issues was the exact opposite of Arnold's beliefs and practices. He did not directly address this in his talk. These departures from the platform have, however, been part of the ongoing discussion about just where Arnold stands on particular issues. For example, the official platform of the Republican party supports President Bush's ban on stem cell research, while Schwarzenegger has taken steps to make California the center of such research, providing funding to attract companies that would develop stem cell projects.

California has not taken steps to ban flag "desecration," but the Republican platform consistently calls for a Constitutional amendment to ban flag burning and desecration and to preserve and respect "Old Glory." A 2002 California state brochure on flags is quite outdated, still listing the display of "red flags" as illegal symbols of anarchy (this law was overturned by the Supreme Court in 1931[3]), but also listing a more current law allowing members of homeowners association to display their flags.

The Republican platform also calls for a Constitutional amendment to ban gay marriages and also a human life amendment to prohibit abortions. But Schwarzenegger supports abortion rights, does not support changing the Constitution because of an issue like gay marriage, and has been quoted as favoring "domestic partnership" arrangements instead.

The Republicans oppose the Kyoto Protocols, which blame global warming on excess carbon emissions. Schwarzenegger, on the other hand, has an active and highly publicized interest in environmental issues and announced in one of his weekly radio addresses that he "signed an executive order to reduce greenhouse gas emissions and make California the leader in the fight against global warming."[4] For Schwarzenegger, there is no doubt that global warming exists and is threatening the environment. He commented, "I say the global warming debate is over. We know the science, we see the threat and we know the time for action is now."[5]

The Republican platform also promotes hunting as a "great American tradition" and gun ownership as a right of the citizens. Arnold acknowledged the interest in hunting in California by designating "Hunter Education Week" to promote hunting safety. He has repeatedly stated his support of the Second Amendment to the Constitution, which gun enthusiasts use to support their "right to bear arms." But Arnold also supports bans on assault rifles and the Brady Bill, which requires a waiting period before gun purchases and safety lock on guns; the Republican platform also promotes "instant" background checks and protection of gun manufacturers from any liability.

The Republican platform promotes abstinence from sexual relations as the way to avoid infection from HIV with very little other commentary about the complexity of the AIDS epidemic in this country. However, California has in place an extensive HIV/AIDS prevention, treatment, and education program that the governor's budgets have continued to support. The Republican platform opposes school-based clinics for reproductive health, as well as mental health counseling, and continues to support school prayer and "school choice," which would pay tuition for students at private and religious schools. Arnold's school focus has been on afterschool programs. He also tried reforming teacher's tenure and pay but not with great success. Schools are also a site to promote his continued interest in fitness. Arnold proudly announced in his State of the State address in January 2006 that "we made our schools healthier by becoming the only state in the union to ban sodas and junk food from our schools."[6] His 2006 budget called for a restoration of art, music, and physical education in California's schools.

So is Arnold a Republican, given all these differences between his political stances and those of the official Republican platform? This was the questioned asked when he first decided to run for governor, but it seemed to have become less of an issue a year later at the Republican National Convention. A Web site called "ArnoldWatch.org," which looks at how special interests seem to be guiding Arnold's political decisions, thinks Arnold is fairly easy to figure out. It reported that Arnold is "pretty much as advertised," according to Bill Whalen from the conservative Hoover Institution. "On social issues, he tends to be progressive to left of center. On economic issues, he tends to be conservative, right of center. Guess where you end up? In the middle, a sort of centrist zero-sum game."[7]

I AM THE AMERICAN DREAM

If Arnold Schwarzenegger seemed at first to be an unlikely speaker at the 2004 Republican National Convention, he quickly established why he was not only a model Republican, but also a model American. He is one of the few appealing figures in the Republican Party who can talk about and embody the American Dream the way Ronald Reagan did. When Arnold stands before the public and states that he has achieved the American Dream, who can argue with him? And when he says he was able to do it because he was a Republican, the story is complete.

Arnold credits Ronald Reagan with reviving the hopes and possibilities of the American Dream. As governor of the same state Reagan governed, Arnold could be seen as continuing the Regan legacy even if the two were far apart on many issues. It was the centrality of the American Dream to both their careers that tied them together. Arnold could also invoke the California version of the American Dream, often called California Dreaming, to reiterate his significance to the concept and to promote himself in the public eye as the dream's incarnation. In his 2006 State of the State address delivered in January 2006, he explained the special form the California Dream takes:

> We must remember that this is the state that represents a dream. If you talk about the Illinois dream or the Delaware dream or the Kentucky dream, no one would know what you meant or what you're talking about. But our dream—the California dream—ah, that means something. People understand it.
>
> It is the means to a better life, where anything is possible— no matter where you came from, no matter who you are. This is what people understand. This is what draws them here. This is why I came here.
>
> So ladies and gentlemen, the state of our state is sound be- cause our dream is sound. Let us commit to building California so that the dream can remain alive for this generation, for the next generation and for generations to come.

The Republican platform for 2004[8] stated an agenda that definitely has Schwarzenegger as its American Dream model. In one portion, Abraham Lincoln is cited as an important figure in Republican history. What Lincoln provided Americans was a vision: "a country united and free, in which all people are guaranteed equal rights and the opportunity to pursue their dreams." The theme of pursuing and fulfilling American dreams is repeated several times as a major issue facing Americans: "[O]ur children deserve to grow up in an America in which all their hopes and dreams can come true," states the introduction, while a later section states the goal of making "the American dream accessible to Native Americans."

Communities are defined as groups of Americans "advancing toward the realization of their dreams," while the Republicans are credited with taking "great strides in making the dream of ownership available to millions of Americans," even naming some programs the American Dream Downpayment Act and Zero Downpayment Mortgages. Education should produce children who are "full of dreams for the future."

The purpose Arnold served, then, at the Republican National Convention was as the literal embodiment of the American Dream that only the Republicans say they can deliver. Despite the fact that Schwarzenegger's positions were inconsistent with much of the party platform, he still closely identified with this promise of being a Republican: that you would achieve the American Dream, especially the parts associated with material well-being.

Arnold Schwarzenegger has called himself the "the living, breathing incarnation of the American Dream."[9] But a speaker at the Democratic National Convention that same year made similar claims on the American Dream, only with a Democratic twist. Barak Obama, currently the only African American (his father was from Kenya) serving in the U.S. Senate, gave a rousing keynote address in July 2004 in Boston.[10] Obama talked about the life of his grandfather and father in Kenya:

> My grandfather had larger dreams for his son. Through hard work and perseverance my father got a scholarship to study in a magical place, America, that's shown as a beacon of freedom and opportunity to so many who had come before him.

Like Arnold, he had an odd-sounding name and he explained that too:

> My parents shared not only an improbable love; they shared an abiding faith in the possibilities of this nation. They would give me an African name, Barack, or "blessed," believing that in a tolerant America, your name is no barrier to success.

And also like Arnold, he claimed the American Dream, but his dream is not the same as the Republican version:

> That is the true genius of America, a faith in simple dreams, an insistence on small miracles; that we can tuck in our children at night and know that they are fed and clothed and safe from harm; that we can say what we think, write what we think,

without hearing a sudden knock on the door; that we can have an idea and start our own business without paying a bribe; that we can participate in the political process without fear of retribution; and that our votes will be counted—or at least, most of the time.

He reiterated the idea many times that a Democratic dream involves taking care of each other:

It is that fundamental belief—it is that fundamental belief—I am my brother's keeper, I am my sisters' keeper—that makes this country work. It's what allows us to pursue our individual dreams, yet still come together as a single American family: "E pluribus unum," out of many, one.

The two speeches, one by the Republican Arnold Schwarzenegger and one by the Democrat Barak Obama, could not be more different, yet each was claiming the right to represent America and its dreams.

Arnold was successful doing this for the Republicans, but it was more than just good rhetoric. Arnold, the epitome of the Republican version of the American Dream, is perhaps first and foremost a money magnet for the Republicans. He has raised millions of dollars not only for his own political agenda, but also for other Republican candidates and for the party. He has drawn contributors from his Hollywood and business connections; two of Arnold's top contributors are *Terminator* director James Cameron and bodybuilding mogul Joe Weider.[11]

THE REPUBLICAN DREAM

The mark of a leader in the mode of Ronald Reagan and both George Bushes is to take the concepts of the American Dream and find ways to apply them to situations not only at home, but in other cultures. For Reagan it was to end the cold war, the hostilities that developed between the United States and communist countries after World War II. For both Bushes it was exporting an American way of seeing the world to Iraq and other countries of the Middle East.

As governor of California and leader of a world-class economy, Arnold has the opportunity to begin his crusade of spreading the Republican version of the American Dream and its economic rewards. During a 6-day trade mission to China in November 2005, Arnold gave a speech at Tsinghua University in Beijing at which he said:

[T]oday I want to talk to you a little bit about the dreams, about the dreams of your future, and dreams for this country. I want to talk to you a little bit about dreams, because it seems to me that I'm somewhat of an expert in dreams, because I had a lot of my dreams become a reality.

He then gives the story of his life and a few minutes later concludes:

[M]y dreams made me successful.
A person, of course, should not be stingy with their dreams. So I, of course, don't just think and dream about myself, but I also have dreams for you, and dreams for China.

One week later, President George Bush visited China for two days to discuss trade issues affecting the entire country, but none of his speeches discussed the American Dream. Arnold had set himself apart as the Republican keeper of the dream.

NOTES

1. See http://newyorkmetro.com/nymetro/news/rnc/9740/.

2. See http://www.pbs.org/newshour/vote2004/repconvention/tuesday.html.

3. See *Stromberg v. California*, 283 U.S. 359 (1931): http://www.law.cornell. edu/supct/html/historics/USSC_CR_0283_0359_ZD1.html.

4. See http://www.governor.ca.gov/state/govsite/gov_htmldisplay.jsp?sFilePath=/ govsite/press_release/2005_06/20050611_GAAS23705_Radio_Global_Warming. html&sCatTitle = Press%20Release.

5. Ibid.

6. See   http://www.governor.ca.gov/state/govsite/gov_htmldisplay.jsp?BV_S essionID=@@@@1384191117.1142803959@@@@&BV_EngineID=cccdaddh fklmklgcfngcfkmdffidfng.0&sCatTitle=Speeches&sFilePath=/govsite/selected_ speeches/20060105_StateoftheState.html&sTitle=2006&iOID=73545.

7. See http://www.arnoldwatch.org/articles/articles_000497.php3.

8. "2004 Republican Party Platform: A Safer World and a More Hopeful America": http://www.gop.com/media/2004platform.pdf.

9. American Media, Inc., *Arnold: The American Dream* (Boca Raton, FL: American Media, Inc., 2003), p. 93.

10. See http://www.washingtonpost.com/wp-dyn/articles/A19751–2004Jul27. html.

11. Some of the top contributors were invited to a fundraiser to support Arnold's re-election as governor. See the invitation at http://www.consumerwatchdog.org/ corporate/rp/5983.pdf.

Chapter 9

THE TERMINATOR AND THE CANDIDATE

Arnold was advised to hang up his leather jacket after the third installment of the Terminator film series came out. The aging action figure's *Terminator 3: Rise of the Machines* came into theaters on July 2, 2003. This movie had a whopping budget of $175 million, more than most other films in history. It took in only $150 million in U.S. ticket sales but more than made up for it with a worldwide figure of $418 million. Video/DVD rental and sales and related merchandise brought in millions more. The combined gross revenues from the three Terminator films is well over $1 billion. When you bear in mind that Arnold takes home a percentage of that in addition to his multi-million dollar salary, you get an idea of just how profitable it had been for Arnold to be the Terminator.

But financial gain was only half the benefit of having become the Terminator. One month after the American release of T3, Arnold announced his run for governor of California. Americans were about to see the Terminator transform the political landscape. The character of the Terminator and all the things he has come to represent was a determining factor in making Arnold Schwarzenegger the dominant figure in California in the fall of 2003. It can easily be argued that in California and around the world, it was actually the Terminator running for governor, not just the Austrian bodybuilder and actor named Arnold.

Arnold has repeatedly said that everyone would like to be a terminator, someone who could get the job done.[1] He has also said, "I like the Terminator ... I'd like to be as resolved as he was and have that kind of power."[2] Terminator director James Cameron took the idea even further, claiming, "There's a bit of the terminator in everybody. In our private fantasy world we'd all like to be able to walk in … and just have our way every minute … People don't cringe in terror from the terminator but go with him. They want to be him for that moment."[3]

The original character that Arnold played in *Terminator* was an evil cyborg, one bent on carrying out an assassination mission. Kyle Reese, a human from the future, explains that the machines that have taken over the word have sent one Terminator, looking like Arnold Schwarzenegger, back into the past to eliminate Sarah Connor. Sarah was the woman who would otherwise become pregnant with the son who would grow up to fight, and possibly destroy, the machines. The Terminators were hard to detect, and only the barking German Shepherds of the underground resistance were able to quickly identify one. They were violent, determined, and they could not be stopped. The original Terminator was described by Reese as "an infiltration unit … part man, part machine. Underneath it's a hyper-alloy combat chassis, microprocessor controlled, fully armored, very tough. But outside it's living human tissue, flesh, skin, hair, blood, grown for the cyborgs."

There were 7 years between the first Terminator movie and the sequel, *Terminator 2: Judgment Day*. It was a testament to Arnold's ability to challenge public expectations and to grow into new and surprising roles that in 1991 he turned the tables completely on America's vision of the Terminator. The cyborg, who began as a force of evil, returned in T2 to serve humanity, not destroy it.

In T2, Arnold was now the *good* guy, sent to protect Sarah and John Connor rather than destroy them. However, as a young John Connor (Sarah's son) is dismayed to learn, the new kinder and gentler Terminator has retained none of the memories of the first Terminator and has to learn about humans all over again. Biographer Laurence Leamer reports that when Arnold and *Terminator* director James Cameron met to discuss *T2*, Arnold was surprised when Cameron told him, "The Terminator comes back and he is going to protect John Connor and he doesn't kill anyone." Arnold is reported to have replied, "But *I'm* the Terminator … I have to terminate. That's what the audience wants to see, me kicking in the doors, machine-gunning everyone."[4] But by the end of *T2*, the Terminator has become a father figure to John, has learned to understand emotions, and sacrifices himself to protect the future of humankind.

Arnold's opponent in T2 was a liquid metal cyborg, the T-1000, one that could shape-shift and become pretty much anything it needed to be to track down and kill Sarah Connor and her son. By *Terminator 3*, the shape-shifting enemy cyborg took on the identity of a woman and used flesh-and-blood wiles as much as her robotic powers to attack John Connor. As cyborgs, all the terminators are by definition boundary crossers, characters who confuse identity and expectations. The boundaries crossed by all the Terminator cyborgs are between the future and the past, reality and fantasy, machines and humans, violence and compassion, males and females, objects and people, and perhaps most significantly for Arnold, between film and reality.

Since the first film in 1984, the label "Terminator" has become associated with off-screen Arnold Schwarzenegger himself, not just with a film character. Of course, Arnold is not the first Hollywood figure to become identified with a particular character. To one generation, Humphrey Bogart will always be Rick in *Casablanca* (1942). Clint Eastwood still is, for many people, *Dirty Harry* (1971). Sylvester Stallone has perpetuated his *Rocky* (1976) image, making *Rocky Balboa* in 2006. But nothing that Stallone or Eastwood did in ordinary life successfully blurred the distinction between the man and the character he played in the movies. Arnold was able to do this with the Terminator.

The Terminator is one of those movie characters that has spread widely in the culture, spawning a theme park ride, clothing and costumes, fashion accessories, toys, video games, trading cards, Halloween costumes, and many imitators. He has become a reference point when we want to talk about getting things done and not letting anything get in our way. Like Arnold himself, the Terminator became a useful metaphor that has appeared in numerous ways. For example, sports stars are also often referred to as Terminators. Nancy Reno's friends call her "the Terminator" in women's professional volleyball. Jeff Reardon of the Atlanta Braves is the Terminator of batters for his ability to choke off late-inning rallies. In the 1998 Winter Olympics, Tara Lipinski's unexpected win in figure skating got her christened, "The Taranator," for her aggressive freestyle program, and Austrian skier Hermann Maier was called "The Hermannator" for a similar approach in his sport.

"MY OWN TERMINATOR"

The Terminator is a symbol of uncontrollable violence, as well as focused determination. The Terminator is an example of what anthropologists call a dominant symbol, one that appears in many contexts and forms and, if examined carefully, helps a culture understand itself. These dominant symbols, like baseball or the American flag, can fulfill many needs. They often combine many meanings into one image and along the way provide a kind of lens through which we can peek into how a particular culture—in this case our own—really operates with regard to violence, dominance, politics, power, and belief. It turns out Arnold's Terminator somehow touches upon all of these ideas.

One of the immediate appeals of the original Terminator character is that he was an incredibly clever "gadget" that could do things like run instant background checks on human beings, punch holes in bad guys' stomachs, deploy enormous weapons with his bare hands, instantly learn how to operate any machine or vehicle it encountered, and persist in its quest no matter how many bullets it had to deflect or absorb, amputations it suffered, or fire-storms it had to walk through.

The young John Connor exclaims in a scene in T2 when he learns he can control the Terminator, "Yes! Cool. My own Terminator," which was an easy reaction to understand. This Terminator conducted its business without anger, without frustration, without regret. Americans were fascinated by both the character and by the actor who not only played the Terminator, but who seemed to have all the same characteristics. If both Arnold and director James Cameron are right that people either wanted to have a Terminator at their command or wanted to be a Terminator, then the California election was about to give them one. This was a character voters knew and understood, and by extension, they could believe that they knew that much more about Schwarzenegger himself. It was this sense of familiarity with Arnold-the-Terminator that compelled voters to take Schwarzenegger's candidacy for California governor so seriously.

TOTAL RECALL

Few elections in U.S. history, whether local, state or national, have received as much attention as the 2003 California recall election did. The entire event, from the types of candidates to the issues and the personal and political controversies, seemed to fascinate most of the world during the fall of 2003. On October 7, 2003, the people of California not only ousted an old governor and elected a new one, but they also made history by conducting one of the oddest, funniest, most dramatic and most provocative elections ever staged.

A recall is a decision by the voters to throw out of office before the end of their term someone who has been rightfully elected to that office. A recall may occur for any number of reasons in each of the 26 states that has such a recall provision. California has had a recall provision in its constitution since 1911, and since then, 31 attempts had been made to recall governors. No previous attempt to get a recall on the ballot had ever been successful.

But no previous California governor had had quite so many different detractors, and despite Governor Davis' denunciation of the recall effort as "sour grapes," the petition to try recalling him was successful, garnering many more than the required 897,158 valid signatures. Since the recall election did not require a traditional primary election where candidates are chosen by their political parties, the process of applying to be a candidate became a free-for-all. All that was needed for someone to declare themselves a valid candidate was a petition with 65–100 signatures and a $3,500 filling fee. If candidates didn't have even that much money, they could submit additional signatures in lieu of payment.

The result was that more than 500 people filed to run for governor, 135 of whom were ultimately certified to run and to be listed on the ballot. This hodge-podge of candidates came to be dubbed, "The Freak Show" because they represented all sorts of odd, fringe groups, as well as some pretty staid and stuffy ones, with a few minor celebrities thrown in. The list of candidates included a retired meat packer, an adult movie actress, a former child star, a billboard icon, an Indian leader, a denture maker, a marijuana lawyer, a gay rights activist, two students, six teachers, five engineers, a gay rights attorney, a cigarette retailer, a prizefighter, a guy named Michael Jackson, another guy named Edward Kennedy, someone named Bob Dole, two doctors, several scientists, a Vietnamese radio producer, a middle weight sumo wrestler, a bounty hunter, a golf pro, a firefighter, a used car dealer, and a man who always dressed all in blue. It was hard for the more serious candidates like Arianna Huffington and Tom McClintock to win much attention in that crowd. Ultimately, though, it didn't matter; Candidate Arnold's 30-plus years in the spotlight left all his opponents in the shadows.

Arnold's Terminator provided a strangely familiar, almost reassuring figure among a collection of freaky one-issue characters, oddball busybodies, and worn out celebrities. Throughout his brief and intense campaign, Arnold was able to keep the attention focused on his goal to be Gray Davis's "term-eliminator," receiving 3,743,393 votes (49%), more than a million more votes than the next runner-up, Lieutenant Governor Cruz Bustamante. From the moment he cleverly announced his candidacy on Jay Leno's *Tonight Show*, Arnold had everyone, ranging from the mainstream TV, radio, and print media to the most edgy Web site producers, comedians, and political commentators, seriously addressing his "Running Man" status. No other credible candidate could afford to ignore him.

That the Terminator became the framework for Arnold's election was evident in the news coverage of the campaign. Domestic newspapers, radio programs, Web sites, and television coverage reinforced the idea that it was the Terminator who was running for governor of California, not merely a movie star. As one reporter put it, "Schwarzenegger's political experience is exactly zero … But as an incarnation of his on-screen presence, he is unbeatable."[5] Across America, it was definitely the Terminator running for and winning the statehouse in Sacramento. Another commentator said, "He is the Terminator, an outsider who'll keep on coming until he has completed his mission: saving the human race from the Democrats."[6] In an article on the Internet entitled, "'The Terminator' Wins California Governorship," the Web site VH1.com predicted, "No doubt Hollywood will eventually make a movie out of this bizarre, dramatic escapade, and it won't be too hard to secure Arnold Schwarzenegger to play the lead role."[7] Like the relentless Terminator himself, the candidate locked onto the target: the statehouse in Sacramento.

Journalists who reported state politics had a lot more work to do covering 135 candidates, but much of their attention was focused on Arnold. After three weeks of campaigning, however, they started complaining to Arnold's staffers that there had been no serious discussions with Arnold about the issues important to the state's citizens and no in-depth interviews with any of the state's newspapers. "What's the rationale for not engaging in serious discussions with journalists who cover California government and politics?" asked one journalist. Confronted by a groups of journalists after Arnold once again avoided their questions at a campaign stop, the staffer explained that, "This is an unconventional campaign that will not necessarily follow the conventions the journalists that cover California politics daily thinks should be dictated to him."[8]

Arnold used the Terminator's unique characteristics—determination, single-mindedness, power, ambiguity, and a no-nonsense approach—in his speeches and his demeanor. He promised to do simple, straightforward things like the Terminator would: terminate waste, terminate taxes, terminate the current governor. Using catch phrases and lines from his movies, Arnold launched one of the strangest and most effective political campaigns. He was going to "terminate" bad policies and politicians; he was going to say "Hasta la vista" to his detractors; this would be a "Total Recall" of California's bad policies.

In his speeches he deployed a variation of these phrases: "Gray Davis has terminated hope. Gray Davis has terminated opportunity. Now it is time to terminate Gray Davis." In the single candidates' debate in which he agreed to participate, he sarcastically offered the argumentative candidate Arianna Huffington a role in his next movie, "T4," presumably a role that included another female opponent being stuffed into a toilet. *Newsweek* magazine described the combination Arnold was employing as "one part 'Terminator 3' and one part 'Meet the Press.'"

Political cartoons often showed the Terminator as a candidate for governor. In one cartoon his cyborg face is damaged to reveal the mechanics underneath, and he is saying to a frightened Gray Davis, "Get out!" In another the Terminator is giving a speech and using all of Arnold's movie titles as parts of his sentences. In many of the other cartoons, he has the Terminator's signature sunglasses.

If international headlines are any indication of the way this election was perceived, then the world also thought that America's most populous state was going to be run by a movie action figure. The *Toronto Star* published the headline "Terminator Wants to Be Governor." The London *Financial Times* had a headline stating, "Terminator 4: Arnie's Victory Is a Triumph of Populism over An Incumbent." "Enter the Terminator," claimed a newspaper in Pakistan; and in Australia, "Terminator Wins Toughest Battle." By the end of the election, one headline announced, "Arnold Poised to Terminate Davis"; it was equally true that Californians—and much of the world—were poised to see the Terminator take over.

When he occasionally strayed from the Terminator-like messages, it rang an odd note. At the end of his statewide bus tour, he said he would clean up state government and wielded a broom. The reference and prop didn't, at least at first, make sense in the context of the rest of the campaign that usually had him warning, "Hasta la vista, Gray Davis" and at the end of his talks, "Thank you and I'll be back." But the would-be Governor was, it turns out, staying in character by using the weapon-of-the-hour, in this case a "loaded" broom, to promise termination of his opponents. Somehow, Arnold had managed to harness both the destructive powers of the original Terminator and the more humane characteristics of his subsequent Terminator roles, to produce yet another variation of himself: the Terminator of California's troubles.

RUNNING MAN

Biographer Nigel Andrews claims Arnold's campaign "was endearing if you believed in the American Dream" and "frightening if you believed in the American nightmare, as represented for many by the election three years before of the policy-vague but folksy and eager-to-please George W. Bush over charisma-free but experienced and hard-headed Al Gore."[9] It was, to say the least, a remarkable moment in American politics. As Andrews put it, "Now here was the human megalith who megaphoned every sound bite, tramped on everyone's sensibilities wittingly or unwittingly, allegedly molested women, led a midterm assault on a democratically elected Democrat and still asked America to love him. And for some reason they did."[10]

During the 8 weeks of the recall campaign, both gleeful comedians and sober reporters filled the airwaves with imitations of Ah-nuld's Austrian accent. Late night comedians provided commentary that was often more critical and insightful than many of the standard news programs. Conan O'Brien joked that, "Earlier today, Arnold Schwarzenegger criticized the California school system, calling it disastrous. Arnold says California's schools are so bad that its graduates are willing to vote for me."[11] The California recall was also an inspiration to the thousands of who flooded the Internet with satires, animations, manipulated images, joke lists, songs, faux film posters, and blogs. The election became one of the most significant shared cultural events of the year and served as further confirmation of the enormous national footprint Arnold had made in the United States.

TERMINATING THE BARBARIAN

For those who still wonder how Arnold Schwarzenegger could have persuaded millions of people to vote him into one of the most powerful elected positions in the country in the most populous and wealthy state in the Union, they only need to be reminded of Arnold's Master Plan. John Milius, Arnold's director in *Conan the Barbarian,* pointed out that Arnold had "always said he's going to be governor of California someday … This is part of his plan, you know."[12]

Part of that plan had to include putting to rest any idea that he was anything like the barbarian he portrayed in the movies, that his admitted use of steroids during his bodybuilding career was not an issue, or that his reputation as muscle-giant did not mean that he possessed an inadequate intellect. Early on, he had important people vouching for him. In 1991, Rabbi Marvin Hier, dean of the Simon Wiesenthal Center, which is dedicated to tracking down Nazi war-criminals, listed three reasons why Arnold would be a good governor: He hates to fail, he's a workaholic, and he started out poor and can still remember those days. "Too many politicians," Rabbi Hier noted, "don't come from that sort of background and forget the important things to strive for."[13]

That the dean of the Simon Wiesenthal Center would speak so glowingly of Arnold told Arnold's detractors that Arnold Schwarzenegger had successfully transcended his father's Nazi past, as well as his birth-nation's anti-Semitism. When President George Bush (senior) named Arnold as Chair of the President's Council on Physical Fitness, the message was clear that Schwarzenegger's steroid use decades earlier was simply part of a vague history that no one need recall. Of course, his marriage to Maria Shriver served to dispel any ideas that he was "uncivilized" like Conan the Barbarian. And Arnold's tremendously successful investments have helped to show him to be a man with considerable brain power and business acumen.

One thing could have brought down Arnold's campaign, the same thing that tarnished the otherwise impressive presidency of Bill Clinton. Accounts of Arnold's sexual misconduct had circulated in Hollywood for years and began to appear in the Los Angeles press right before the election. He was accused of being crude and sexist with female co-workers, accused by 16 women of groping or harassing them in a demeaning way. Yet the allegations did not undo Arnold's campaign. Two days before the election, the *Los Angeles Times* printed a commentary by Susan Faludi entitled "Conan the Vulgarian," in which she demanded to know "Why are so many not offended?"[14] Why didn't the accusations do more to undermine Arnold's credibility with voters?

One reason may be that while one of Arnold's most popular phrases is "I'll be back," his true motto, according to *Flex* magazine, is "Don't look back."[15] Always looking ahead, Arnold was able not only to ignore the facts of his own past, but also to persuade Californians and Americans in general to overlook or forgive those past actions. Despite the allegations of "groping" and harassment, Schwarzenegger's vision of his future hardly ever wavered. With complete conviction, after he issued a mild apology for offending people, he and Maria Shriver presented him as the right man for California. None of the criticisms leveled at his past were sufficient to undermine his mission. Arnold, like the Terminator, had too much momentum to be stopped.

ON THE ROAD TO SACRAMENTO

A few days before the October 7, 2003 vote, Arnold staged an elaborate demonstration that clearly illustrated the appeal of the connection between the on-the-ground person running for governor and the on-the-screen characters from some of his well-known movies. Arnold's campaign chartered a caravan of buses, all named after his movies. "Running Man" and "Total Recall" carried his staff and friends; "Predator" buses were for the media. The four-day tour of the state was called the "California Comeback Express." While none of these busses featured references to the Terminator, the effect was to keep our attention focused on Arnold's movie characters. Like the Terminator, Arnold's characters in *The Running Man*, *The Predator*, and *Total Recall* all were notable for overcoming preposterously difficult obstacles to prevail over their opponent and, in one way or another, to save the world. California voters could be confident that the "running man" in the "total recall" election was the same as the Terminator himself.

The caravan started out in the south, in Orange County, California, a well-known Republican stronghold. Speaking at the Orange County Fairgrounds, Arnold told the public that he intended to make powerful changes in state government. Nearby, there was a large crane from which hung a steel wrecking ball. Looking over at the crane, Arnold told the large cheering crowd at the Orange County Fairgrounds, "In the movies, if I played a character and I didn't like something, you know what I did? I destroyed it." Then to the crowd's delight, the wrecking ball was dropped onto a car, symbolizing the way in which Arnold intended to eliminate, or "terminate," the newly imposed car tax that was one of the major issues in the election. "Hasta la vista, car tax," he proclaimed.

Even before he was elected, Arnold became the "Governator," a play on the words "Terminator" and "governor." "The Governator?" questioned one newspaper back in June 2003. "Recall numbers show Governator about to be real," claimed another news source. The Internet's Urban Dictionary[16] created a forum in which people could post definitions of this new term: "Governator." Like all the definitions in this collective dictionary, the Governator ones were part joke and part critique. Their definitions are revealing about how Arnold was blended with the Terminator character and what people thought of this. A Governator is a "machine sent back in time to terminate Gray Davis ..."; "A ruthless cyborg killing machine (Schwarzenegger) created by SkyNet (Republican Party) ... to kill our founding fathers before they can write our Constitution ..."; "A robotic groping machine sent back from the future to terrorize womankind"; "The killer machine sent into the depths of time to overtake the evil that is Gray Davis and restore political safety to California."

As candidate for Governor, Arnold made a point of identifying himself with the Terminator who could destroy his political opponents. The fact that so many others had picked up on this fusion of Arnold and the relentlessly destructive Terminator suggests that this movie character has worked its way into everyday speech, thoughts, imagination, and circumstances. Nearly half the state's voters chose Arnold. Whether it was because his rhetoric was compelling, his fame mesmerizing, his physical presence still seductive, his famous wife persuasive, the other candidates simply too ridiculous, or because the attacks against him simply backfired, Arnold Schwarzenegger became the most famous governor in the world.

NOTES

1. Bill Zehme, "Mr. Big Shot," *Rolling Stone*, August 22, 1991, p. 42.

2. K.W. Woods, *Schwarzenegger: Muscleman to Terminator* (Lincolnwood, IL: Publications International, 1991), p. 6.

3. Sean French, *The Terminator* (Berkeley: University of California Press, 1996), p. 39.

4. Laurence Leamer, *Fantastic: The Life of Arnold Schwarzenegger* (New York: St. Martin's Press, 2005), pp. 231–232.

5. Oren Rawls, "In Other Words …" *Forward*, August 15, 2003: http://www.forward.com/issues/2003/03.08.15/otherwords.html.

6. See John Sutherland, "T4: Rise of a Governor," August 11, 2003. Accessed July 26, 2006. http://www.theage.com.au/articles/2003/08/08/1060145859748.html.

7. See http://www.vh1.com/news/articles/1479631/20031008/schwarzenegger.

8. This exchange can be seen in the video documentary *How Arnold Won the West*, Dir. Alex Cooke. Article Z (Paris), Mentorn (London), 2005.

9. Nigel Andrews, *True Myths: The Life and Times of Arnold Schwarzenegger* (London: Bloomsbury, 2003), p. 243.

10. Ibid, p. 247.

11. See http://politicalhumor.about.com/library/blschwarzeneggerjokes.htm.

12. Bill Zehme, "Mr. Big Shot," *Rolling Stone*, August 22, 1991, p. 41.

13. Aaron Latham, "Schwarzenegger as California Governor?" M *inc.* (October 1991): 115.

14. Susan Faludi, "Conan the Vulgarian," *Los Angeles Times*, October 5, 2003, p. M1.

15. Peter McGough, "Anatomy of an American Icon," *FLEX* (July 1997): 64.

16. See http://www.urbandictionary.com.

Chapter 10

GOVERNOR ARNOLD

For people around the country and around the world—political analysts, fans, skeptics, and fellow politicians—the magic of the California recall election was precisely that the victor was what one media strategist called "a huge new leader."[1] At first the celebrity factor was important. As the executive director of Sacramento's Downtown Partnership (representing hundreds of property and business owners in the area), Michael Ault commented that "this governor is going to bring us a celebrity cachet."[2]

The October 23, 2003, headline of the *Los Angeles Times* online edition read, "Schwarzenegger's Star Power Glows at the Capitol."[3] A California Highway Patrol spokesman declared, "It's all Arnold all the time around here," and the California state Senate's chief-sergeant said, "Everybody wants a look at him."[4] But Arnold set a different agenda from his first day in office. Just as significant as the peoples' reaction was Arnold's own perspective on his new role. "Today is a new day in California," he declared. "My administration is not about politics. It is about saving California."[5]

FIRST YEAR IN OFFICE

On November 17, 2003, in front of a huge crowd of adoring voters and fans, Arnold Schwarzenegger was sworn in as California's Governor. In his inaugural address, he defined the fiscal crisis he felt California was suffering. It would require fixing deficit spending, the worker's compensation system, and other devastated aspects of the economy. Using bodybuilding metaphors he declared:

What we face may look insurmountable. But I learned something from all those years of training and competing. I learned something from all those sets and reps when I didn't think I could lift another ounce of weight.

What I learned is that we are always STRONGER than we KNOW. CALIFORNIA is like that, too.

We are STRONGER than we KNOW.

There's a massive weight we must lift off our state.

Alone, I cannot lift it. But TOGETHER, we CAN.[6]

That same day he issued an executive order rescinding the increase in the unpopular "car tax" that his predecessor put into effect. He also signed orders halting the hiring of new state employees and the signing of any new state contracts. Later he repealed a law giving driver's licenses to illegal immigrants and developed a plan to borrow $15 million to deal with the state's deficit. But he was also criticized for proposing a state budget that cut funds for education, for transportation, for the poor, disabled and mentally ill, and for health care. Governing the world's sixth largest economy isn't really much like being a cinematic action star or the king of the bodybuilding world. Arnold would soon discover that it is much more difficult to lift a state out of its troubles than it is to lift barbells over his head.

At his inaugural, Arnold also made this bold and simple statement: "I enter this office beholden to NO ONE except YOU, my fellow citizens. I pledge my governorship to YOUR interests, not to special interests."[7] Yet immediately after taking office, Arnold became a prolific fundraiser for both Republican causes and for the ballot measures he was preparing for a November 2005 election. Arnold got accused of "cash-register politics" because he did not hesitate to take funds from drug companies, insurance companies, and real estate developers. As one critic complained, "Just when he was having trouble filling theatres at $8 a seat, he found an audience he could entertain who would pay $21,100 a seat"[8] at his fundraisers.

California has always been know as a state where business-as-usual meant that special interest groups had a lot of influence on how the state made its laws and spent its money. So when Arnold promised to disrupt business-as-usual, he had to address the special interest group problem. Along the way he redefined a special interest group in such a way that he outraged numerous groups in the state and did nothing to disrupt years of influence peddling.

The issue of just who is defined as a special interest dogged him for months. As one reporter explained the problem, "During his campaign, he initially said he wouldn't accept any campaign money from outside sources. He later amended his pledge to say he wouldn't take money from special interests, then narrowed the definition of special interest to public employee unions, Indian gaming tribes and single-issue trade associations."[9]

The most striking example of his misstep in dealing with the problem of special interest groups in California was to take on the state's nurses. The California Nurses Association had worked for 12 years to get laws passed that established safe levels of Registered Nurses-to-Patient Ratios, a formula that established nursing staffing in medical facilities. California was the first state to do this and was widely praised for its efforts. Governor Schwarzenegger attempted to roll back the agreement, and the nurses fought back, staging more than 100 protests in the next year. At the December 2004 Governor's Conference on Women and Families, the nurses protested loudly, and Arnold advised the 10,000 women present not to listen to them because they were a special interest group "who don't like me because I'm always kicking their butt." This led to a yearlong court battle that the nurses finally won, but not before Arnold's redefinition of special interest groups, which he also extended to teachers and firefighters, was ridiculed and used to defeat some of his legislative agendas.

Other problems developed in the first year. Arnold had to find a way to pay local governments around the state the billions of dollars they lost when, as promised, he repealed the increase in the vehicle license fee. His method was to use his executive authority to steer nearly $3 billion to these local governments, a tactic that effectively left the state legislature out of the process. Members of the legislature were, understandably, disturbed. Although Arnold had promised a bi-partisan discussion of issues and problems, he was also using a heavy hand by going around the legislature and directly to the people when he wanted something done. In March 2004, he got two propositions passed: Prop. 57, which let him borrow the $15 million he needed to help the state, and Prop. 58, which required the state to have a balanced budget each year. He also provided the muscle to push for a bill requiring the casinos owned and controlled by Native Americans to begin paying their "fair share of gaming revenues."[10]

In Arnold's first State of the State address in January of 2004, just a few months on the job, he joked, "OK, I changed my mind. I want to go back to acting." But he was quick to reassure his constituents—and his detractors—that California was on the rise again. "We have a new spirit, a new confidence. We have a new common cause in restoring California to greatness."[11]

In a speech at a shopping mall in July of 2004, one of many he made around the state to sell his ideas directly to the people, Arnold called the Democratic legislators who could not agree on a state budget "girlie men." He repeated the phrase again when he addressed the Republican National Convention in November 2004, and on both occasions the comments got widespread publicity. According to Arnold's spokesman, the use of the phrase was a tactic by Arnold to express his frustration at the legislators, not an attempt to question their sexual orientation.[12]

By the end of Arnold's first year as Governor, Californians still overwhelmingly approved of the job he was doing. *The Sacramento Bee* noted that while Arnold's approval ratings were a remarkable 70% after year-one, "He's been an OK governor, demonstrably more engaged and effective than the hapless Davis, but he hasn't yet tackled and conquered the state's most intractable political issues."[13] In his efforts to raise the state out of deep debt, Arnold actually increased the spending and the debt.

While individual politicians might like Arnold personally, the Democrat-controlled legislature fought Arnold on many bills and proposals. In turn, Arnold vetoed many of the bills put forward by the Democrats. Some politicians and analysts found Schwarzenegger's boldness to be refreshing, or at least interesting. Democratic mayor of Los Angeles, James K. Hahn said, "We haven't seen this kind of bold leadership in Sacramento for a long, long time, and we are really grateful for it."[14] The Governator was already demonstrating how he intended to run California his way.

VETERAN GOVERNOR

In his State of the State address in January 2005, Arnold proposed more changes to the way the state did business. He said that reforms were needed in the way teachers were paid, and he proposed drastic changes in the state's pension obligations to its employees. He also hinted at reforms that would be put to the voters, giving the power to set voting districts to a panel of judges instead of the state legislators and giving the governor budget veto power.

When the state officials did not take up his causes, Arnold again decided to go around them. He said in a speech in March 2005, "Well now it's March, 8 weeks since my State of the State, and the legislators have done nothing to address my reforms. No counter-proposals. No special committees. No negotiations to build cooperation. Nothing. All they have offered is a lot of excuses, a lot of complaints and a lot of finger pointing."[15] Arnold called for a statewide special election to be held in November 2005. The purpose of the election was to put into effect political reforms without going through the state legislature.

In August of 2005, fans of the Rolling Stones could purchase a ticket for their Fenway Park concert in Boston for a price of $100,000. For that fee, 40 affluent fans got to sit with Governor Schwarzenegger in his luxury box. This was just one of the many unique fundraising efforts the Arnold team put together toward raising the money to finance Arnold's statewide campaign for reform, which would eventually cost the state $50 million to conduct.

Arnold proposed four initiatives (Props. 74–77) of the eight that were on the ballot. Stated simply, they were, "to have teachers work for five years, not two, before getting tenure; to require unions to ask each individual member before using their dues for political campaigns; to put a cap on state spending; and to put retired judges, not legislators, in charge of redrawing electoral districts."[16] The first would make it easier to fire teachers, the second would neutralize the political clout of unions, the third would give the governor almost complete control over the state budget, and the fourth would take power away from the state legislators. No one seemed willing to grant Arnold these extensive powers, and all the initiatives were defeated, at least in part due to the efforts of the teachers, nurses, firefighters, and public employees he had insulted over the past year.

The defeat of these initiatives was taken as an indication that Arnold had to face the reality of how California worked. As the *Washington Post* commented, "Schwarzenegger's fall from grace this year has been as precipitous as it has been befuddling because his first year in Sacramento was widely called a success."[17] His refusal to grant clemency to convicted murderer Stanley "Tookie" Williams, who was scheduled to be executed in December 2005, showed Arnold how the larger world viewed his decisions. Austrian politicians in Graz were threatening to rename Arnold Schwarzenegger Stadium because the Austrian government is opposed to capital punishment. Arnold's response to this outcry was to write a letter to the mayor of Graz, demanding that his name be removed from the stadium by year's end, "and in the future, the use of my name to advertise or promote the city of Graz in any way is no longer allowed."[18]

SLIPPING IN THE POLLS

By the end of 2005, Arnold's approval ratings had slipped to around 40%. In September 2005, he announced that he would run for re-election in November 2006. Besides the budget issues and his fall in popularity, immigration was becoming a major political issue. Thousands of illegal immigrants, many of whom work on California's farms and in its homes, staged demonstrations during the spring of 2006. Arnold had made several statements about immigrants, including an editorial in the *Wall Street Journal* that asked for a federal policy that developed "legislation based on a simple philosophy: control of the border ... and compassion for the immigrant"[19] He opposes making illegal immigration a felony as the federal legislators were suggesting.

Arnold won the Republican Primary for the 2006 gubernatorial election with 90% of the votes. He will face Democratic Candidate Phil Angelides, who is State Treasurer, a native of Sacramento, and a former real estate developer. Like Arnold, Angelides is a multimillionaire, and the race has become a media extravaganza with expensive ad campaigns across the state. Arnold also faces one very powerful Republican candidate: the "old" Arnold Schwarzenegger—the one Californians so passionately elected—the Terminator. In one of Angelides ads, a Terminator is shown riding a motorcycle backwards. The voice-over says, "Backwards? It's Schwarzengger who's taking us backwards." If the current Governor Arnold pales in the face of that action hero, he may not carry the state for a second term. One California journalist predicts, "California will remain an Arnold vehicle,"[20] but election day 2006 will set Arnold's political future.

NOTES

1. David K. Li, "Pumped Arnie Dumps the Gov," *The New York Post*, October 8, 2003, p. 6.

2. Ibid.

3. Jenifer Warren and Shawn Hubler, "Schwarzenegger's Star Power Glows at the Capitol," *Los Angeles Times*, October 23, 2003, p A21.

4. Ibid.

5. Adam Tanner, "Schwarzenegger Becomes Calif. Gov., Seeks 'New Day,'" *Reuters* online, November 17, 2003. Accessed January 2006, http://news.yahoo.com/news?tmpl=story2&cid=578&u=/nm/20031117/ts_nm/politics_california_dc&printer=1.

6. See http://www.governor.ca.gov/state/govsite/gov_htmldisplay.jsp?BV_SessionID=@@@@1456742697.1145236364@@@@&BV_EngineID=ccchaddhidgkjgicfngcfkmdffidfog.0&sCatTitle=Speeches&sFilePath=/govsite/selected_speeches/20031117_SwearingIn.html&sTitle=2003&iOID=53503.

7. Ibid.

8. See http://www.arnoldwatch.org/press_releases/press_releases_000524.php3.

9. See http://www.arnoldwatch.org/articles/articles_000221.php3.

10. Ibid.

11. "Governor Schwarzenegger Delivers First State of the State Address," January 6, 2004: http://www.schwarzenegger.com/en/life/hiswords/words_en_stateOstate.asp?sec=life&subsec=hiswords.

12. John M. Broder, "Schwarzenegger Calls Budget Opponents 'Girlie Men,'" *New York Times*, July 19, 2004, p. 11.

13. Dan Walters, "Governor Is Still Popular, But Capitol Remains Recalcitrant," *Sacramento Bee*, November 17, 2004. Retrieved from http://www.sacbee.com/content/politics/columns/walters/story/11449815p-12364069c.html.

14. Ibid.

15. See http://www.governor.ca.gov/state/govsite/gov_htmldisplay.jsp?BV_SessionID=@@@@0433184809.1145247748@@@@&BV_EngineID=cccjaddhidgldihcfngcfkmdffidfng.0&sCatTitle=Speeches&sFilePath=/govsite/selected_speeches/20050301_GovernorGoestothePeople.html&sTitle=2005&iOID=61518.

16. See http://www.time.com/time/nation/article/0,8599,1127699,00.html.

17. See http://www.washingtonpost.com/wp-dyn/content/article/2005/11/05/AR2005110501343.html.

18. Gary Delsohn, "Schwarzenegger Demands His Name Pulled from Austrian Stadium," *Sacramento Bee*, December 19, 2005, p. A3.

19. See http://www.opinionjournal.com/editorial/feature.html?id=110008209.

20. Joe Matthews, "Arnold Realizes He's Too Famous." *The New Republic* online, October 21, 2005. Retrieved from http://www.tnr.com/doc.mhtml?i=2005103105&s=mathews103105.

Chapter 11

PRESIDENT ARNOLD

At the end of each campaign stop during the California recall election, and many times since then as governor, Arnold has uttered the catch phrase that will be forever associated with his most famous movie character: "I'll be back." The catch phrase has found its way into the everyday live of Americans across the country. Each of the millions of repetitions of the phrase calls to mind the steely determination and unstoppable power of Arnold Schwarzenegger. This was all fun and games when Arnold stayed in the world of movie Terminators, but translated into politics it becomes something else.

In some ways, the phrase is an apt description of Arnold's life so far and maybe even a prediction of its future. "I'll be back" takes on a special significance when we look at Arnold's history of recovering from failures or defeats or being temporarily removed from the spotlight. Those scripted cinematic words embody the very real approach Arnold has used to recover from setbacks and to reinsert himself into the American mainstream over and over again. Many times in his various careers, Arnold has been called a has-been, someone who had seen better days, someone whose career or influence or charisma was fading. These analyses were not entirely wrong, but what Arnold did that was different was to spawn a new career, a new sphere of influence that took off as one endeavor faded and another was yet to be realized.

Through a variety of incarnations, Arnold has remained a near constant fixture in the media for nearly 40 years. Even before his bodybuilding days started to fade, Arnold was beginning to conquer Hollywood and was already a fledgling real-estate tycoon. His flexibility and vision served him well in several arenas over time. When his films seemed to generally have become undistinguished action stories (*Red Heat* 1988) or outright failures (*Last Action Hero* 1993 or *Junior* 1994) he was already on his way to becoming friendly with politicians around the country. When his action hero days seemed over, he still came back with one last ironic turn as the Terminator in *Terminator 3* (2003), right before he ran for governor.

But where does a man go who has achieved so much in one lifetime? Where does the path lead whose stepping stones have included teen bodybuilding championships, national and international bodybuilding stardom, Hollywood celebrity, real estate tycoon status, national fitness czar appointment, and high-profile political office? What will it look like when Arnold comes back next time?

HIGHER OFFICE?

There has been much speculation that a U.S. presidential run is a logical next step. As the governor of California, Arnold has been refining his leadership skills as he leads a state that has a bigger economy than most countries around the world. He is taking the case of California and its economic develop to the international scene, making quite a splash in China and Israel as he attempts to sell investments in the California and American Dreams.

The Governator has already been called "The Presidator" in news stories across the world, and this has been going on for some time. One of the first speculations was meant to be a funny comment back in 1984, the year the first terminator movie came out. The *New York Times* joked that year that if presidential contests were more like beauty pageants, "Arnold Schwarzenegger could become president."[1] Since 1984, in fact, the elections have increasingly emphasized the popular appeal of the candidates rather than their political views, very much like beauty pageants. "President Schwarzenegger?" asked the *San Francisco Chronicle* right after the recall election; only by 2003, it did not have to be asked as a joke.

Of course, the great seer, Sylvester Stallone, had also predicted a presidency in Arnold's future. In the movie *Demolition Man* (1993), set in the year 2026, Stallone stars as John Spartan, a Los Angeles cop who was purposely frozen as a punishment. After being awakened, Spartan drives along with Lt. Lenina Huxley (Sandra Bullock) and sees a sign for the President Schwarzenegger Library. Lenina explains that 30 years earlier Arnold Schwarzenegger had been elected president of the United States. She elaborates that "Even though he was not born in this country, his popularity at the time caused the 61st Amendment." Stallone, who worked in the movies at the same time as Arnold and with the same emphasis on his body and funny accent, was unable to take any of his well-known movie characters (like Rocky or John Rambo) and turn them into incredible wealth and tremendous political clout. While Arnold is continually expanding his influence and power, Stallone is reviving his Rocky character for one last boxing bout in *Rocky Balboa*. Stallone's greatest legacy may be Rocky's triumphant run up the steps of the Philadelphia Museum of Art, which people imitate everyday in Philadelphia but which doesn't inspire those same people to support him in politics or business.

Arnold himself has slyly resisted dismissing the idea, letting everyone speculate about whether this is his true ambition. For the man who claims to have achieved the American dream, is this the only piece missing from the perfect life? Arnold is a "naturalized" citizen of the United States because he was born in a foreign country and later chose voluntarily to become a U.S. citizen. At present, the U.S. Constitution does not permit a foreign-born citizen to become president. This is stated in Article II, Section 1, clause 5 of the Constitution:

> No person except a natural born citizen, or a citizen of the United States at the time of the adoption of this Constitution, shall be eligible to the Office of President; neither shall any person be eligible to that office who shall not have attained the age of thirty-five years, and been fourteen years a resident with the United States.

There is a historic reason for this prohibition being added to the Constitution, which was ratified in 1787 and took effect in 1789. At the time of the American Revolution, there was concern that foreign powers would try to install a leader in the colonies whose real loyalties lay with a foreign government. The clause in the constitution has never been tested, and the definition of a natural born citizen has been shown to be complicated over the years. But in Arnold's case it is clear that he is currently not eligible to become President of the United States.

CONSTITUTIONAL AMENDMENT?

While that would seem an insurmountable obstacle for the Austrian Oak, a number of senators and congressmen have proposed legislation to amend the Constitution to allow for naturalized citizens born in foreign lands to become the supreme American leader. It is not inconceivable that within Arnold's lifetime such an amendment will pass, enabling him to run for the highest office in the United States. There is no reason to believe that his role as governor will not have a remarkable sequel. That Arnold Schwarzenegger cannot, at this time, be elected president of the United States should not be seen as a permanent condition.

On February 29, 2000, Representative Barney Frank of Massachusetts introduced a joint resolution to the U.S. House of Representatives requesting an amendment to the U.S. Constitution. The proposed amendment would make eligible for the Office of the President any person who has been a citizen for 20 years. Being foreign born would no longer make someone ineligible for the presidency. Frank's position was that "the essential premise of this constitutional provision is that there is some reason to distrust the complete patriotism of people who were born elsewhere, and I have not found that to be the case as a general rule."[2] The proposal did not go very far, perhaps because there were others in the year 2000 who agreed with one witness who said, "I could give what I consider the definitive argument against the proposed amendment in two words: Arnold Schwarzenegger."[3]

On July 10, 2003, even before Arnold formally announced his candidacy for governor of California, his friend and political ally, Senator Orrin Hatch of Utah, proposed a joint bill that would begin the process of amending the constitution to allow foreign-born citizens to be eligible to run for president after they had been citizens for 20 years.[4] Hatch coined a catchy name for his amendment, the "Equal Opportunity to Govern Amendment." It is also called the "Hatch Amendment" as well as the "Arnold Amendment." Hatch explained even before Arnold got elected, in a talk at the National Press Club on October 3, 2003, "If Arnold Schwarzenegger turns out to be the greatest governor of California, which I hope he will, if he turns out to be a tremendous leader and he proves to everybody in this country that he's totally dedicated to this country as an American ... we would be wrong not to give him that opportunity,"[5] The National Constitution Center in Philadelphia has been inviting visitors to its Web site and its museum building to cast their votes for and against the idea.[6] "Give 'Terminator' a shot at the White House?" asked the Utah News.[7]

On September 15, 2004, Representative Dana Rohrabacher from California introduced the House of Representative's counterpart bill to Hatch's Senate bill. Rohrabacher commented that "Today we have many significant political leaders who cannot be president simply because they were not born here. California Governor Arnold Schwarzenegger is the most famous example, but what about Michigan's Governor, Jennifer Granholm, who came to the United States from Canada at the age of four? Or Congressman Pete Hoekstra, who came to this country when he was a mere three years old and has been given the responsibility of being Chairman of the House Permanent Select Committee on Intelligence? Congressman Hoekstra oversees the intelligence community in a post-9/11 United States and yet regardless of his lifetime of service, he cannot be President."[8]

There have been at least a dozen serious efforts to have this law changed before. A constitutional amendment requires that two-thirds of the members of each house of Congress, the Senate and the House of Representatives, vote in favor of the amendment. Then it has to go to each state for ratification. Three quarters of the states, or 38 of them, have to approve the amendment before it becomes law. The process can be long and often fails. *USA Today* reported that some think it is only Arnold's celebrity that keeps the discussion going:

> "Only Schwarzenegger's charisma has kept an amendment from being hooted down," says John Smolenski, an assistant professor of history at the University of California-Davis. "The idea that this would even be on the table is purely a testament to him."[9]

Several organizations have sprouted up around the subject, with two specifically supporting Arnold's potential as a presidential candidate. The first group, which ran television ads in California, is called "Amend US,"[10] and their ads encourage amending the constitution for Arnold. The group is organized by supporters of Arnold's gubernatorial campaign. One ad the group has run says "Help us amend for Arnold and 12 million other Americans." More recently, their Web site has added the name of Jennifer Granholm, and it is now "Amend for Arnold and Jen."

The second group has begun a petition drive[11] called "Arnold Schwarzenegger for President." Their goal is 20 million signatures to be sent to Orrin Hatch to show support for his amendment. The online petition has so far garnered less than 1,000 signatures. Some of these signature will undoubtedly be called into question since the T-1000 Terminator from Alpha Centauri, convicted murderer Charles Manson, dictator Joseph Stalin, Osama Bin Laden from Kabul, Kentucky, Adolph Hitler, and Adolph Hitler's girlfriend Eva Braun were among the supposed signers.

The petition is sponsored by two UCLA grads who call themselves "Operation Arnold." Their Web site, OperationArnold.com, states a desire to have "America Undivided-One Nation United," not a catchy phrase but one that is supposed to show their bi-partisan approach. On the petition they state:

> Through a bi-partisan effort, Operation Arnold's mission is to promote and encourage the American Dream and the hope that lies within each and every American. Arnold Schwarzenegger is living proof that if you believe in freedom and accept the great responsibility that comes with it, the impossible can become possible through hard work and perseverance. We are dedicated to showing Americans that Arnold's dreams truly are Our dreams and that there is a hero like Arnold in all of us.[12]

Much of the rest of the Web site of Operation Arnold seems to be a promotion for a self-published book on the issues and merchandise saying "Prezinator," "Dreams are Heavier than Weights," "Determinator," and "I'll be backed," all carrying on with the name puns and catch phrases that have made Arnold a part of our everyday lives.

USA Today also reported Arnold's reaction to all this:

> In April, he said in a joking manner that he would run if the opportunity arose. At an international travel-industry show in Los Angeles, he said, "I thank you very much for changing the Constitution of the United States of America, and I accept your nomination to run for president." Pause. "Oh, wrong delegation. Sorry, wrong speech."[13]

He has appeared in several interviews saying he supports the idea of the amendment. For detractors, this would have to be Arnold's best sales job yet, and even greater fears of "Hasta la vista, democracy" have been voiced.[14] Maria Shriver has come out in favor of the change to the Constitution even though she does not think it will happen.

There is an unattributed quote on the Arnold Schwarzenegger for President petition that says, "The only thing bigger than Arnold himself is the American Dream."[15] Despite the difficulties of changing the constitution and convincing people that Arnold will not turn America into a dictatorship, this sentiment may turn out to be the driving force behind the next step in the amazing American Dream journey of Arnold Schwarzenegger.

NOTES

1. Sydney H. Schanberg, "Mondale Has Great Legs," *New York Times*, May 19, 1984, p. 23.

2. See http://thomas.loc.gov/cgi-bin/query/z?c106:H.J.+Res.+88.

3. See http://commdocs.house.gov/committees/judiciary/hju67306.000/hju67306_0.HTM.

4. See http://www.congress.gov/cgi-bin/query/z?c108:S.J.RES.15.

5. Christopher Smith, "Put Past to Rest, Hatch says of Arnold," *The Salt Lake Tribune*, October 4, 2003, p. A4.

6. See http://capwiz.com/constitutioncenter/issues/alert/?alertid = 6788591& type = ML.

7. See http://deseretnews.com/dn/view/0,1249,510039949,00.html.

8. See http://www.congress.gov/cgi-bin/query/D?r108:2:./temp/~r108FZi1PO.

9. See http://www.usatoday.com/news/politicselections/2004–12–02-schwarzenegger-amendment_x.htm.

10. See http://www.amendus.com/Default.aspx.

11. See http://www.thepetitionsite.com/takeaction/684216123?ltl = 1141754019#body.

12. Ibid.

13. See http://www.usatoday.com/news/politicselections/2004–12–02-schwarzenegger-amendment_x.htm.

14. See http://www.buzzflash.com/farrell/03/08/19.html.

15. See http://www.thepetitionsite.com/takeaction/684216123?ltl = 1145638774.

EPILOGUE: YODA VS THE TERMINATOR

If the Terminator had to fight Yoda, who would win? This was a question posed to Arnold Schwarzenegger by a fan and Arnold answered it on his Web site. Fearing at first that the question was just a joke, Arnold decided to answer it anyway because it gave him a chance to make a statement about the principles that have always governed his life. He saw parallels between himself and Yoda that may at first seem hard to accept.

The 900-year-old Yoda, a wise and powerful Jedi Master in the *Star Wars* universe, had a greater command of the Force than most Jedi. The Force is a type of energy field both inside and outside living beings. It binds the Galaxy together. Yoda was a great combatant despite his diminutive stature and could overcome any opponent using his light saber or his Jedi abilities derived from the Force.

Likewise for Arnold Schwarzenegger, known first and foremost for his majestically built, over-muscled body, it is actually the mind that is more important and more powerful. Throughout his life, Arnold also employed a kind of force to keep his life plan on track and to achieve his many goals. His force was derived from determination and discipline. In bodybuilding, which has all the appearances of being just about how a contestant looks physically, Arnold was famous for using psychology to diminish his opponents' confidence and enhance his own presentation. Through his later years in the movies and in politics, Arnold was able to use the force of his personality and his celebrity to make deals and get things done.

Arnold acknowledged that to become a Jedi Master, Yoda had to have a "strong, serious mind and a disciplined will." This, Arnold explained, is just like the commitment of an actor or a bodybuilder:

> I couldn't have done any of it without commitment, and that takes discipline and willpower first. The mind is actually more powerful than the body, because it is our will that helps us shape everything else around us, whether it's our careers, how we help our communities or even if it's just making time for our families.[1]

Arnold concedes, then, that Yoda would be the winner in a showdown between the Jedi Master and the Terminator, but not, it seems, between Yoda and Arnold. While the Jedi Master might win in a mind-over-matter contest, Arnold made sure to add, "but I'm sure I'd kick his butt in a pose-down!"[2]

This determination to turn every potential defeat into victory has been one of Arnold's most powerful defining character traits throughout his career and across his life. This is why, for the past four decades, Arnold Schwarzenegger has been a major "Force" in the intersecting universes of bodybuilding, show business, fitness, financial investment, and politics.

If Yoda is the Jedi Master, then Arnold is the Image Master. Since the 1960s, he has managed, with unmatched success, to keep positive and flattering images of himself—as the great pumper of iron, as the Terminator, as Conan the Republican, as the Governator, and maybe later as the Prezinator—in the eyes and minds of fans and detractors alike. You could argue that Arnold's showmanship has, for many years, been politically motivated, or you could make the case that Arnold's political career is, first and foremost, showmanship. You could place Arnold's body of work in the context of his persistent passion to achieve greatness; it's just as fair to say his passion for greatness has always also been the work of his body. This biography of Arnold Schwarzenegger has been a fantastic journey into the life of a national and international star who has had a galaxy-sized influence on our collective imaginations.

NOTES

1. See "Ask Arnold," *Schwarzenegger.com*, http://www.schwarzenegger.com/en/news/askarnold/news_askarnold_eng_legacy_441.asp?sec=news&subsec=ask arnold.

2 Ibid.

FURTHER READING

Andrews, Nigel. *True Myths: The Life and Times of Arnold Schwarzenegger*. New York: Carol Publishing Group, 1996.

Blitz, Michael, and Louise Krasniewicz. *Why Arnold Matters: the Rise of a Cultural Icon*. New York: Basic Books, 2004.

Butler, George. *Arnold Schwarzenegger: A Portrait*. New York: Simon & Schuster, 1990.

Flynn, John. *The Films of Arnold Schwarzenegger*. Secaucus, NJ: Carol Publishing Group, 1993.

Fussell, Samuel Wilson. *Muscle: Confessions of an Unlikely Bodybuilder*. New York: Perennial, 1991.

Gaines, Charles. *Stay Hungry*. Garden City, NY: Doubleday, 1972.

Gaines, Charles, and George Butler. *Pumping Iron: The Art and Sport of Bodybuilding*. New York: Simon & Schuster, 1974.

Green, Tom. Arnold! *The Life of Arnold Schwarzenegger*. New York: St. Martin's Press, 1987.

Heywood, Leslie. *Bodymakers: A Cultural Anatomy of Women's Bodybuilding*. Rutgers, New Brunswick: Rutgers University Press, 1998.

Leamer, Laurence. *Fantastic: The Life of Arnold Schwarzenegger*. New York: St. Martin's Press, 2005.

Leigh, Wendy. *Arnold: An Unauthorized Biography*. Chicago: Congdon & Weed, 1990.

Paris, Bob. *Gorilla Suit: My Adventures in Bodybuilding*. New York: St. Martin's Press, 1997.

Schwarzenegger, Arnold, with Bill Dobbins. *The New Encyclopedia of Modern Bodybuilding*. New York: Simon and Schuster, 1998.

Schwarzenegger, Arnold, with Bill Dobbins. *Arnold's Bodybuilding for Men.* New York: Simon & Schuster, 1981.

Schwarzenegger, Arnold, and Douglas Kent Hall. *Arnold: The Education of a Bodybuilder.* New York: Simon & Schuster, 1977.

Schwarzenegger, Arnold, and Douglas Kent Hall. *Arnold's Bodyshaping for Women.* New York: Simon & Schuster, 1979.

Schwarzenegger, Arnold, with Charles Gaines. *Arnold's Fitness for Kids (Ages 11–14).* New York: Doubleday, 1993.

Shriver, Maria. *Ten Things I Wish I'd Known—Before I Went Out into the Real World.* New York: Warner Books, 2000.

Watson, B.S. *Arnold Schwarzenegger* (Unauthorized Biography). Chicago, IL: Kidsbooks, Inc., 1992.

Wayne, Rick. *Muscle Wars: The Behind the Scenes Story of Competitive Bodybuilding.* New York: St. Martin's Press, 1985.

Zannos, Susan. *Arnold Schwarzenegger: A Real-Life Reader Biography.* Bear, DE: Mitchell Lane Publishers, 1999.

INDEX

ABOUT THE AUTHORS

LOUISE KRASNIEWICZ is a Senior Research Scientist in the American Section at the University of Pennsylvania Museum of Archaeology and Anthropology. She is the co-author of *Why Arnold Matters: The Rise of a Cultural Icon* (2004).

MICHAEL BLITZ is Professor of English and Chair of Interdisciplinary Studies at John Jay College of Criminal Justice of the City University of New York. He is the co-author of *Why Arnold Matters: The Rise of a Cultural Icon* (2004).

3M